To the Reader:

Scientology® applied religious philosophy contains pastoral counseling procedures intended to assist an individual to gain greater knowledge of self. The mission of the Church of Scientology is a simple one: to help the individual achieve greater self-confidence and personal integrity, thereby enabling him to really trust and respect himself and his fellow man. The attainment of the benefits and goals of Scientology philosophy requires each individual's dedicated participation, as only through his own efforts can he achieve these.

This book is based on the religious literature and works of the Scientology Founder, L. Ron Hubbard. It is presented to the reader as part of the record of his personal research into life, and the application of same by others, and should be construed only as a written report of such research and not as a statement of claims made by the Church or the Founder.

Scientology philosophy and its forerunner, Dianetics® spiritual healing technology, as practiced by the Church, address only the "thetan" (spirit). Although the Church, as are all churches, is free to engage in spiritual healing, it does not, as its primary goal is increased spiritual awareness for all. For this reason, the Church does not wish to accept individuals who desire treatment of physical or mental illness but prefers to refer these to qualified specialists of other organizations who deal in these matters.

The Hubbard® Electrometer is a religious artifact used in the Church confessional. It in itself does nothing, and is used by ministers only, to assist parishioners in locating areas of spiritual distress or travail.

We hope the reading of this book is only the first stage of a personal voyage of discovery into this new and vital world religion.

Church of Scientology International

This Book Belongs to:

_____

_____
(Date)

THE DYNAMICS OF LIFE

L. RON HUBBARD

THE DYNAMICS OF LIFE

Bridge
PUBLICATIONS, INC.

Published in the U.S.A. by
Bridge Publications, Inc.
4751 Fountain Avenue
Los Angeles, California 90029

ISBN 0-88404-343-6

Published in other countries by
New Era® Publications International, ApS
Store Kongensgade 55
1264 Copenhagen K, Denmark

ISBN 87 7336-587 4

Printed in the United States of America

Dianetics spiritual healing technology is man's most advanced school of the mind. *Dianetics* means "through the soul" (from Greek *dia*, through, and *noos*, soul). *Dianetics* is further defined as "what the soul is doing to the body." It is a way of handling the energy of which life is made in such a way as to bring about a greater efficiency in the organism and in the spiritual life of the individual.

Important Note

In reading this book, be very certain you never go past a word you do not fully understand.

The only reason a person gives up a study or becomes confused or unable to learn is because he or she has gone past a word that was not understood.

The confusion or inability to grasp or learn comes AFTER a word that the person did not have defined and understood.

Have you ever had the experience of coming to the end of a page and realizing you didn't know what you had read? Well, somewhere earlier on that page you went past a word that you had no definition for or an incorrect definition for.

Here's an example. "It was found that when the crepuscule arrived the children were quieter and when it was not present, they were much livelier." You see what happens. You think you don't understand the whole idea, but the inability to understand came entirely from the one word you could not define, *crepuscule*, which means twilight or darkness.

It may not only be the new and unusual words that you will

have to look up. Some commonly used words can often be misdefined and so cause confusion.

This datum about not going past an undefined word is the most important fact in the whole subject of study. Every subject you have taken up and abandoned had its words which you failed to get defined.

Therefore, in studying this book be very, very certain you never go past a word you do not fully understand. If the material becomes confusing or you can't seem to grasp it, there will be a word just earlier that you have not understood. Don't go any further, but go back to BEFORE you got into trouble, find the misunderstood word and get it defined.

Definitions

As an aid to the reader, words most likely to be misunderstood have been defined in footnotes the first time they occur in the text. Words sometimes have several meanings. The footnote definitions in this book only give the meaning that the word has as it is used in the text. Other definitions for the word can be found in a dictionary.

A glossary including all the footnote definitions is at the back of this book.

Editors' Foreword

L. Ron Hubbard originally wrote this work as the first formal record of his research and discoveries into the function of the human mind. He did not publish it at that time, but offered it to friends who copied it and redistributed it. In this manner the manuscript found its way around the world, creating a groundswell of interest in Dianetics techniques and prompting a flood of questions, letters and requests for further data.

Recently, the original manuscript for this work was located. The text has been meticulously compared to the manuscript to ensure that this edition is a complete rendition of what the author intended for publication.

It is with great pride that we present to you this new edition of L. Ron Hubbard's *The Dynamics of Life*.

—The Editors, 1989

Contents

Introduction

In 1932 an investigation was undertaken to determine the dynamic principle of existence[1] in a workable form which might lead to the resolution of some of the problems of mankind. A long research in ancient and modern philosophy[2] culminated, in 1938, in the heuristically[3] discovered primary law. A work was written at that time which embraced[4] man and his activities. In the following years further research was undertaken in order to prove or disprove the axioms[5] so established.

Certain experiences during the war made it necessary for the writer to resolve[6] the work into applicable equations and an intensive program was begun in 1945 toward this end.

---

1. **dynamic principle of existence:** is *Survive!* No behavior or activity has been found to exist without this principle. It is not new that life is surviving. It is new that life has as its entire dynamic urge only survival.

2. **philosophy:** the love or pursuit of wisdom, or of knowledge of things and their causes, whether theoretical or practical.

3. **heuristically:** in a manner serving to find out; specifically applied to a system of education under which the student is trained to find out things for himself.

4. **embraced:** included; contained.

5. **axioms:** statements of natural laws on the order of those of the physical sciences.

6. **resolve:** to change or transform.

A year later many techniques had been discovered or evolved and a nebulous[7] form of the present work was formulated. Financed chiefly by a lump-sum disability compensation, that form of Dianetics was intensively applied to volunteer subjects and the work gradually developed to its present form.

Dianetics has been under test by the writer, as here delineated,[8] for the past four years. The last series of random volunteers, numbering twenty, were rehabilitated, twenty out of twenty, with an average number of work hours of 151.2 per subject. Dianetics offers the first anatomy[9] of the human mind and techniques for handling the hitherto[10] unknown reactive mind,[11] which causes irrational and psychosomatic[12] behavior. It has successfully removed any compulsions,[13] repressions,[14] neuroses[15] and psychoses[16] to which it has been applied.

L. R. H.
January, 1948

7. **nebulous:** unclear; vague; indefinite.

8. **delineated:** explained in words; described.

9. **anatomy:** the structure of an animal or plant or any of its parts.

10. **hitherto:** until this time.

11. **reactive mind:** the portion of the mind which works on a stimulus-response basis (given a certain stimulus it will automatically give a certain response) which is not under a person's volitional control and which exerts force and power over a person's awareness, purposes, thoughts, body and actions.

12. **psychosomatic:** *psycho* refers to mind and *somatic* refers to body; the term *psychosomatic* means the mind making the body ill or illnesses which have been created physically within the body by derangement of the mind.

13. **compulsions:** irresistible, repeated, irrational impulses to perform some act.

14. **repressions:** commands that the organism must not do something.

15. **neuroses:** emotional states containing conflicts and emotional data inhibiting the abilities or welfare of the individual.

16. **psychoses:** conflicts of commands which seriously reduce the individual's ability to solve his problems in his environment to a point where he cannot adjust some vital phase of his environmental needs.

1

Primary Axioms

1

Primary Axioms

Dianetics is a heuristic science built upon axioms. Workability rather than idealism has been consulted. The only claim made for these axioms is that by their use certain definite and predictable results can be obtained.

The principal achievement of Dianetics lies in its organization. Almost any of its parts can be found somewhere in history, even when they were independently evolved by the writer. There are no principal sources, and where a practice or a principle is borrowed from some past school[1] the connection is usually accidental and does not admit any further use or validity of that school. Dianetics will work, and can only be worked, when regarded and used as a unity. When diluted by broader applications of older practices, it will no longer produce results. To avoid confusion and prevent semantic[2] difficulties, new and simplified terminology has been used and is used only as defined herein.

Dianetics is actually a family of sciences. It is here addressed

---

1. **school:** a group of people held together by the same teachings, beliefs, opinions, methods, etc.

2. **semantic:** of or pertaining to meaning, especially meaning in language.

in the form of a science of thought applicable to psychosomatic ills and individual aberrations.[3]

The field of thought may be divided into two areas which have been classified as the "knowable" and the "unknowable." We are here concerned only with the "knowable." In the "unknowable" we place that data which we do not need to know in order to solve the problem of improving or curing of aberrations of the human mind. By thus splitting the broad field of thought, we need not now concern ourselves with such indefinites as spiritualism, deism,[4] telepathy,[5] clairvoyance[6] or, for instance, the human soul.

Conceiving this split as a line drawn through the area, we can assign a dynamic principle of existence to all that data remaining in the "knowable" field.

After exhaustive research one word was selected as embracing the finite[7] universe as a dynamic principle of existence. This

---

3. **aberrations:** departures from rational thought or behavior. From the Latin, *aberrare*, to wander from; Latin, *ab*, away, *errare*, to wander. It means basically to err, to make mistakes, or more specifically to have fixed ideas which are not true. The word is also used in its scientific sense. It means departure from a straight line. If a line should go from A to B, and it is "aberrated" it would go from A to some other point, to some other point, to some other point, to some other point, to some other point and finally arrive at B. Taken in its scientific sense, it would also mean the lack of straightness or to see crookedly as, for example, a man sees a horse but thinks he sees an elephant. Aberrated conduct would be wrong conduct, or conduct not supported by reason. Aberration is opposed to sanity which would be its opposite.

4. **deism:** belief in the existence of a God on purely rational grounds without reliance on revelation or authority; especially, the 17th and 18th century doctrine that God created the world and its natural laws, but takes no further part in its functioning.

5. **telepathy:** communication between minds by some means other than sensory perception.

6. **clairvoyance:** the ability to perceive things that are not in sight or that cannot be seen.

7. **finite:** having measurable or definable limits.

word can be used as a guide or a measuring stick and by it can be evaluated much information. It is therefore our first and our controlling axiom.

The first axiom is:

Survive!

This can be seen to be the lowest common denominator[8] of the finite universe. It embraces the conservation of energy, all forms of energy. It further delineates the purpose of that energy so far as it is now viewable by us in the "knowable" field. The activity of the finite universe can easily be seen to obey this axiom as though it were a command. All works and energies can be considered to be motivated by it. The various kingdoms[9] have this as their lowest common denominator, for animals, vegetables and minerals are all striving for survival. We do not know to what end we are surviving, and in our field of the "knowable" and in our choice of only the workable axioms, we do not know and have no immediate reason to ask why.

All forms of energy are then surviving to some unknown end, for some unknown purpose. We need only to know that they *are* surviving and that, as units or species, they *must* survive.

By derivation from the first workable axiom, we come into possession of the second. In obedience to the command *survive*, life took on the form of a cell which, joining with other cells, formed a colony. The cell, by procreating,[10] expanded the colony.

---

8. **common denominator:** a characteristic, element, etc., held in common.

9. **kingdoms:** the three great divisions into which all natural objects have been classified (the animal, vegetable and mineral kingdoms).

10. **procreating:** bringing (a living thing) into existence by the natural process of reproduction.

The colony, by procreating, formed other colonies. Colonies of different types united and necessity, mutation[11] and natural selection[12] brought about specializing which increased the complexity of the colonies until they became an aggregation.[13] The problems of the colonial aggregation were those of food, protection and procreation. In various ways a colonial aggregation of cells became a standardized unity and any advanced colonial aggregation came into possession by necessity, mutation and natural selection, of a central control system.

The purpose of the colonial aggregation was to survive. To do this it had to have food, means of defense, protection and means of procreation. The control center which had developed had as its primary command, *survive!* Its prime purpose was the food, defense, protection and means of procreation.

Thus can be stated the second workable axiom:

The purpose of the mind is to solve problems relating to survival.

The ultimate success of the organism, its species or life would be, at its unimaginable extreme, immortality. The final failure in obedience to the law *survive* would be death. Between eternal survival and death lie innumerable gradations. In the middle ground of such a scale would be mere existence without hope of much success and without fear of failure. Below this

---

11. **mutation:** change or alteration in form.

12. **natural selection:** a process in nature resulting in the survival and perpetuation of only those forms of plant and animal life having certain favorable characteristics that best enable them to adapt to a specific environment.

13. **aggregation:** a group, body or mass composed of many distinct parts.

point would lie, step by step, innumerable small errors, accidents, losses, each one of which would tend to abbreviate[14] the chances of reaching the ultimate goal. Above this point would lie the small successes, appreciations and triumphs which would tend to secure the desirable goal.

As an axiom, the mind can then be said to act in obedience to a central basic command, *survive,* and to direct or manage the organism in its efforts to accomplish the ultimate goal for the individual or species or life, and to avoid for the individual or species or life any part of the final failure, which leads to the stated axiom:

The mind directs the organism, the species, its symbiotes[15] or life in the effort of survival.

A study of the field of evolution will indicate that survival has been, will be and is the sole test of an organism, whether the organism is treated in the form of a daily activity or the life of the species. No action of the organism will be found to lie without the field of survival, for the organism is acting within its environment upon information received or retained, and error or failure does not alter the fact that its basic impulse was motivated by survival.

Another axiom may then be formulated as follows:

The mind as the central direction system of the body, poses,[16] perceives and resolves problems of survival and directs or fails to direct their execution.

---

14. **abbreviate:** to shorten by cutting off a part; to cut short.

15. **symbiotes:** any or all life or energy forms which are mutually dependent for survival.

16. **poses:** puts forward, presents.

As there are many organisms in the same species, all attempting to accomplish the same end, and as there are many species, and as matter itself is attempting in one unit form or another to survive, there is necessarily conflict and contest amongst the individuals of the species, species or units of matter. Species cannot survive without being interested primarily in the species. Natural selection and other causes have established this as a primary rule for survival: *That the unit remain alive as long as possible as a unit and, by association and procreation, that the species remain alive as a species.* Second-grade interest is paid by the unit or the species to its symbiotes. Third-grade interest is paid to inanimate[17] matter. As this is apparently the most workable solution, natural selection best preserves those species which follow this working rule. And the symbiotes of the successful species therefore have enhanced opportunity for survival.

Man is the most successful organism currently in existence, at least on this planet. Man is currently winning in the perpetual cosmic[18] election which possibly may select the thinker of the new *thought.*

Man is heir to the experience and construction of his own ancestors. As cellular conservatism is one of the factors of survival, his brain is basically the same brain which directed and resolved the problems of his animal forebears.[19] By evolution and natural selection, this brain therefore has the primary priority in emergencies. Superimposed[20] on this animal brain has been developed an enormously complex analyzer, which probably exists in his frontal lobe.[21]

17. **inanimate:** (of rocks and other objects) lifeless, (of plants) lacking animal life.

18. **cosmic:** of the universe.

19. **forebears:** ancestors.

20. **superimposed:** laid or placed (a thing) on top of something else.

21. **frontal lobe:** portion of the brain behind the forehead.

The command, *survive,* is variable in individuals and species to the extent that it may be strong or weak. Superior strength of the command in the individual or species is normally, but variably, a survival factor. The primary facet[22] of personality is the basic strength of the *dynamic* drive.

The *dynamic* is variable from individual to individual and race to race. It is varied by physiology,[23] environment and experience. Its manifestation[24] in the animal brain effects the tenacity[25] of the individual to life or purpose, and it effects the activity of the analyzer. The first characteristic of the individual which should be considered is the basic strength of his *dynamic.* By this an axiom can be formulated:

The persistency of the individual in life is directly governed by the strength of his basic dynamic.

The analytical, human or, as it has elsewhere been called erroneously, the conscious mind, is variable from individual to individual and race to race in its ability to perceive and resolve problems. Another axiom can then be formulated:

Intelligence is the ability of an individual, group or race to resolve problems relating to survival.

It should be noted that there is a distinct difference between the *dynamic* and the intelligence. High intelligence may not

---

22. **facet:** any of a number of sides or aspects, as of a personality.

23. **physiology:** the organic processes or functions of an organism or any of its parts.

24. **manifestation:** something which is apparent to the senses; something which shows itself.

25. **tenacity:** the quality or state of being persistent or stubborn.

denote[26] high *dynamic*. High *dynamic* may not denote high intelligence. *Intelligence* is mental sensitivity and analytical ability. *Dynamic* is the persistency of the individual in obedience to the command, *survive!*

It has been noted that there is a gradation in the scale of survival. Gains toward the ultimate goal are pleasurable. Failures toward the final defeat are sorrowful or painful. Pleasure is therefore the perception of well-being, or an advance toward the ultimate goal. Pain, therefore, is the perception of a reduction toward the final defeat. Both are necessary survival factors.

For the purpose of Dianetics, *good* and *evil* must be defined. Those things which may be classified as *good* by an individual are only those things which aid himself, his family, his group, his race, mankind or life in its dynamic obedience to the command, modified by the observations of the individual, his family, his group, his race or life.

As *evil* may be classified those things which tend to limit the dynamic thrust of the individual, his family, his group, his race or life in general in the dynamic drive, also limited by the observation, the observer and his ability to observe.

Good may be defined as constructive. *Evil* may be defined as destructive—definitions modified by viewpoint. The individual man is an organism attempting to survive in affinity or contest with other men, races and the three kingdoms. His goal is survival for himself, his progeny,[27] his group, his race, his symbiotes, life and the universe in general in contest with any efforts or entities which threaten or impede his efforts to attain the goal.

---

26. **denote:** be a sign of; indicate.

27. **progeny:** children, descendants or offspring collectively.

12

His happiness depends upon making, consolidating[28] or contemplating gains toward his goal.

It is a purpose of Dianetics to pass man across the abyss[29] of irrational, solely reactive thought[30] and enter him upon a new stage of constructive progression to the ultimate goal.

28. **consolidating:** making or becoming strong, stable, firmly established, etc.

29. **abyss:** anything too deep for measurement; profound depth.

30. **reactive thought:** identity thought. The reactive mind is distinguished by the fact that although it thinks, it thinks wholly in identities. For instance, to the reactive mind under certain conditions there would be no difference between a microphone and a table.

2

An Analogy of the Mind

2

An Analogy[1] of the Mind

It is not the purpose of Dianetics to reconstruct the human mind. The purpose of Dianetics is to delete from the existing mind those physically painful experiences which have resulted in the aberration of the analytical mind and to restore in its entirety the proper working function of a brain not otherwise physically deranged.[2]

Dianetics *embraces* the various physiological aspects of psychosomatic medicine, including the glandular[3] balance or imbalance of the organism, as influenced by painful physical experiences.

The initial adjustments of the individual are included in Child Dianetics[4] and Educational Dianetics.[5] Surgical and medical procedures as they affect the mind are covered in Medical

---

1. **analogy:** explanation of something by comparing it point by point with something similar.

2. **deranged:** upset in arrangement, order or operation; unsettled; disordered.

3. **glandular:** derived from or affected by organs in the body that secrete substances to be used in other parts of the body or expelled from it.

4. **Child Dianetics:** that branch of Dianetics which is concerned with promoting optimum survival of the immature human organism until such time as standard procedure for adults may be employed.

5. **Educational Dianetics:** contains the body of organized knowledge necessary to train minds to their optimum efficiency and to an optimum of skill and knowledge in the various branches of the works of man.

Dianetics, which is briefly touched upon in this manual. Judicial Dianetics,[6] Political Dianetics[7] and Military Dianetics are elsewhere touched upon or allocated for study. Dianetics, as a family of sciences, proceeds however from the axioms cursorily[8] touched upon in the last chapter and is uniformly governed by the principles of the behavior of the human mind.

When an individual is acting contrary to survival of himself, his group, progeny, race, mankind or life he can be considered to be unintelligent, uninformed or aberrated. *Every single instance of aberrated conduct threatening the general goal of the individual as outlined in the last chapter can be proven to have a source which will specifically be found to be a painful experience containing data not available to the analytical mind.* Every single instance and facet of aberrated conduct has its exact causation in the physically painful error which has been introduced during a moment of absence of the analytical power.

Dianetics consists of discovering the aberration in the individual, finding the physically painful experience which corresponds to it and placing the data therein contained at the disposal of the analytical mind.

More as effort to demonstrate how that is accomplished than as an actual outline of the character of the mind, the following analogy is offered.

---

6. **Judicial Dianetics:** covers the field of judgment within the society and amongst the societies of man. Of necessity it embraces jurisprudence (science or philosophy of law) and its codes and establishes precision definitions and equations for the establishment of equity. It is the science of judgment.

7. **Political Dianetics:** embraces the field of group activity and organization to establish the optimum conditions and processes of leadership and intergroup relations.

8. **cursorily:** in a hastily done manner; done rapidly with little attention to detail.

First there is the physio[9]-animal section of the brain, containing the motor controls, the subbrains[10] and the physical nervous system in general, including the physical aspect of the analytical section of the brain. The control of all voluntary and involuntary muscles is contained in this section. It commands all body fluids, blood flow, respiration, glandular secretion, cellular construction and the activity of various parts of the body. Experimentation has adequately demonstrated this. The physio-animal mind has specific methods of "thinking." These are entirely reactive.[11] Animal experimentation—rats, dogs, etc.—is experimentation on and with precisely this mind and little more. *It is a fully conscious mind and should never be denoted by any term which denies it "consciousness" since there is no period in the life of the organism from conception to death when this mind is not awake, observing and recording perceptics.*[12]

This is the mind of a dog, cat or rat and is also the basic mind of a man so far as its operating characteristics are concerned. A man in the deepest possible somnambulistic[13] sleep is still in possession of more mind and thinking and coordinating ability than a lower animal.

The term *consciousness* is no more than a designation of the awareness of *now*. The physio-animal mind never ceases to be aware of *now* and never ceases to record the successive instances

---

9. **physio:** a portion of a word meaning "physical."

10. **subbrains:** such parts of the body as the "funny bones" or any "judo sensitive" spots: the sides of the neck, the inside of the wrist, the places the doctors tap to find out if there is a reflex. These are subbrains picked up on the evolutionary line.

11. **reactive:** irrational, reacting instead of acting.

12. **perceptics:** sense messages.

13. **somnambulistic:** trancelike.

of *now* which in their composite make up a *time track*[14] connecting memory in an orderly chain.

Cessation of life alone discontinues the recording of perceptions on this orderly track. *Unconsciousness* is a condition wherein the organism is discoordinated only in its analytical process and motor control direction. In the physio-animal section of the brain, a complete time track and a complete memory record of all perceptions for all moments of the organism's existence is available.

As life progresses, for instance, from a blade of grass, greater and greater complexities and degrees of self-determinism[15] are possible. Energy in its various forms is the primary motivator in the lower orders, but as the complexity of the order is increased into the animal kingdom, the physio-animal brain attains more and more command of the entire organism until it itself begins to possess the second section of the mind.

All animals possess in some slight degree an analyzer. This, which we designate the *analytical mind*, is present even in lower orders, since it is only that section of the brain which possesses the self-deterministic coordinative command of the physio-animal brain and thus of the body. In a rat, for instance, it is no more than its "conscious" awareness of *now* applying to lessons of *then* without rationality but with instinct[16] and painful experience. This is the analytical section of the mind in a lower animal but it is the *reactive mind* in a man whose *analytical mind* is so

---

14. **time track:** consists of all the consecutive moments of "now" from the earliest moment of life of the organism to present time.

15. **self-determinism:** a condition of determining the actions of self; the ability to direct oneself.

16. **instinct:** an inborn impulse or tendency to perform certain acts or behave in certain ways.

---

highly attuned[17] and intricate that it can command entirely the physio-animal brain and thus the body.

Man not only possesses a superior physio-animal mind but possesses as well an *analytical mind* of such power and complexity that it has no real rival in any other species. The *analytical mind* of man cannot be studied by observing the reactions of animals under any situations. Not only is it more sensitive but it possesses factors and sensitivities not elsewhere found.

Continuing this analogy: Lying between the *analytical mind* and the physio-animal mind may be conceived the *reactive mind*. This is the coordinated responses of the physio-animal mind, the "analytical" mind of animals and the first post of emergency command in man. All errors of a psychic[18] or psychosomatic nature can be considered for the purposes of this analogy to lie in the *reactive mind*. The first human *analytical mind* took command of the body and physio-animal mind under strained and dangerous circumstances when man was still in violent contest with other species around him. It can be considered that the *analytical mind* received command with the single proviso[19] that instantaneous emergency would be handled by the outdated but faster *reactive mind*.

Any and all errors in thinking and action derive from the reactive mind as it is increased in strength and power by painful experience. It can be called a shadow mind, instantaneously reactive when any of its content is perceived in the environment of the individual, at which time it urgently bypasses the analytical mind and causes immediate reaction in the physio-animal

---

17. **attuned:** adjusted; brought into harmony or agreement.

18. **psychic:** of or having to do with the psyche (the spirit) or mind.

19. **proviso:** a condition or qualification.

mind and in the body. Additionally, the reactive mind is in continual presence when chronically[20] restimulated by a constantly present restimulator—which is to say, an approximation[21] of the reactive mind's content or some part thereof continually perceived in the environment of the organism. The reactive mind is in action so long as it is activated by an exact or nearly exact approximation of its content. But given too continuous a restimulation, it can and does derange both the physio-animal mind and body below it and the analytical mind above it. It was created by deranging circumstances of a physical nature, hence it deranges.

The entire content of the reactive mind is records of physical pain with its accompanying perceptions during disconnection of the analyzer. All aberrated conduct and error on the part of an individual is occasioned[22] by restimulation of his reactive mind.

None of these minds are "unconscious," nor are they subconscious. The entire organism is always conscious but the temporary dispersion[23] of the thought processes of the analytical mind brings about a condition whereby that mind, having been dispersed and considering itself the residence of the person, is unable to obtain and reach data perceived and received by the organism during the analytical mind's condition of dispersion. That the analytical mind can be thrown, by pain or shock, out of circuit is a survival factor of its own: as sensitive "machinery" it must be protected by a fuse system.

---

20. **chronically:** in a continuing manner; constantly.

21. **approximation:** a state of coming or getting close to or resembling.

22. **occasioned:** caused; brought about.

23. **dispersion:** state or condition of being scattered, driven or sent in different directions.

3

The Dynamics

3

The Dynamics

The basic dynamic, **survive!** increases in complexity as the complexity of the organism evolves. Energy may be considered to have taken many paths through eternity to arrive intact at the infinite goal. The "why" of the goal may lie above the finite line but below it, demarked[1] by the word *survive!* definite manifestations are visible. Energy collects into various forms of matter which collect and aggregate in various materials and compounds. Life evolves from the simplest basic into complex forms since evolutionary change is in itself a method of survival.

Conflict amongst species and individuals within the species is additionally a survival factor. Affinity of individuals for groups, races and the whole of its species, and for other species, is additionally a survival factor, as strong or stronger than conflict.

Drive is defined as the dynamic thrust through time toward the attainment of the goal. Survive is considered to be the lowest common denominator of all energy efforts and all forms. It can then be subdivided specifically into several drive lines as applicable to each form or species. The unaberrated self contains eight main drives which are held in common with man.

---

1. **demarked:** limited or distinguished.

The dynamics are: One, self; Two, sex; Three, group; Four, mankind; Five, life; Six, the physical universe; Seven, thought; Eight, universal thought or theta.[2]

An entire philosophy can be built around each one of these dynamics which will account for all the actions of an individual. Any one of these philosophies is so complete that it can be logically made to include the other seven. In other words, all purpose of an individual can be rationalized[3] into the dynamic of self. A philosophy exists which attempts to rationalize everything into the sexual dynamic, and so on with all the dynamics. Observing that each one can stand as a logical unity, one finds it necessary to retire[4] to the lowest common denominator of the basic dynamic which actually does explain the eight subdivisions. As each one of the subdivisions is capable of supporting the whole weight[5] of a rational argument, it can readily be deduced that each is of nearly equal importance in the individual. The aberrated conditions of a society tend to vary the stress on these dynamics, making first one and then another the keynote[6] of the society.

In an unaberrated individual or society, the validity of all eight would be recognized.

The unaberrated individual may physiologically possess or environmentally stress one or more of these dynamics above the others. In terms of basic personality, the physiological-environmental-educational aspect of the individual is of varied strength in the eight dynamics.

---

2. **theta:** the symbol (Greek letter θ, *theta*) which represents thought, life force, the spirit or soul.

3. **rationalized:** explained or interpreted on rational grounds.

4. **retire:** to return; to come back.

5. **weight:** influence, power or authority.

6. **keynote:** the basic idea or ruling principle.

Each one of the eight dynamics breaks further into purposes which are specific and complex. Purposes and other factors entangle these dynamics, and varying situations and the observational power of the individual may conflict one of these dynamics against another within the individual himself. This is a basic complex factor of unaberrated personality.

I. **The Dynamic of Self** consists of the dynamic thrust to survive as an individual, to obtain pleasure as an individual and to avoid pain. It covers the general field of food, clothing and shelter, personal ambition and general individual purpose.

II. **The Dynamic of Sex** embraces the procreation of progeny, the care of that progeny and the securing for that progeny of better survival conditions and abilities in the future.

III. **The Dynamic of Group** embraces the various units of the species of man, such as the association, the military company,[7] the people in the surrounding countryside, the nation and the race. It is characterized by activity on the part of the individual to obtain and maintain the survival of the group of which he is a part.

IV. **The Mankind Dynamic** embraces the survival of the species.

V. **The Dynamic of Life** is the urge of the individual to survive for life and for life to survive for itself.

VI. **The Physical Universe Dynamic** is the drive of the individual to enhance the survival of all matter, energy, time and space.

---

7. **company:** any relatively small group of soldiers.

VII. **The Thought Dynamic** concerns the urge of the individual to survive as thought.

VIII. **The Dynamic of Universal Thought** is the urge of the individual to survive for the Creator.

While man is concerned with any one of the above dynamics, any one of them may become antipathetic[8] to his own survival. This is *rational conflict* and is normally and commonly incident to survival. It is nonaberrative in that it is rational within the educational limitation.

The family as a unit is not a dynamic but a combination of dynamics. And in this and other societies it attains a position of interest which is not necessarily inherent[9] in the individual or group.

Basically simple, complexity is introduced amongst the dynamics by individual and group irrationalities. The basic (unaberrated) individual has continual difficulty rationalizing the problems of importances and choices amongst these dynamics. When the basic individual becomes aberrated and is attendantly[10] unable to reason freely on all problems, a selection of importances amongst these dynamics becomes nearly impossible and produces aberrated solutions which may resolve[11] such an extreme as the destruction of the individual himself, by himself, under the mistaken solution that he may thus obey the primary command.

---

8. **antipathetic:** opposed or antagonistic in character, tendency, etc.

9. **inherent:** existing in something as a natural or permanent characteristic or quality.

10. **attendantly:** in a manner accompanying as a circumstance or result.

11. **resolve:** to determine or decide upon (a course of action, etc.).

Note: All self-destructive effort is irrationality of a precise nature which will often be found by the auditor[12] in his preclear[13] during auditing[14] but which forms no part of the basic personality of the individual.

---

12. **auditor:** a person trained and qualified in applying Dianetics processes and procedures to individuals for their betterment; called an auditor because *auditor* means "one who listens."

13. **preclear:** any person who has been entered into Dianetics processing. A person who, through Dianetics processing, is finding out more about himself and life.

14. **auditing:** the application of Dianetics processes and procedures to someone by a trained auditor.

4

The Basic Individual

4

The Basic Individual

For the purposes of this work the terms *basic individual* and *Clear* are nearly synonymous since they denote the unaberrated self in complete integration[1] and in a state of highest possible rationality; a *Clear* is one who has become the *basic individual* through auditing.

The precise personality of the basic individual is of interest to the auditor. His complete characteristic is established by:

(1) the strength of his basic *dynamic;* (2) the relative strengths of his dynamics; (3) the sensitivity, which is to say the intelligence, of his analyzer; (4) the coordination of his motor controls; (5) his physiological and glandular condition; (6) his environment and education.

The experiences of each individual also create an individual composite and so may additionally designate individuality. There are as many distinct individuals on Earth as there are men, women and children. That we can establish a common denominator of drive and basic function does not, cannot and will not

---

1. **integration:** the organization of various traits, feelings, attitudes, etc., into one harmonious personality.

alter the fact that individuals are amazingly varied one from the next.

It will be found by experience and exhaustive research, as it has been clinically established, that the basic individual is invariably responsive in all the dynamics and is essentially "good." There are varying degrees of courage but in the basic individual there is no pusillanimity.[2] The virtues[3] of the basic individual are innumerable. His intentional vices[4] and destructive dramatizations[5] are nonexistent. He is cooperative, constructive and possessed of purpose. In short, he is in close alignment with that ideal which mankind recognizes as an ideal. This is a necessary part of an auditor's working knowledge, since deviations from it denote the existence of aberration, and such departures are unnatural and enforced and are no part of the self-determinism of the individual.

Man is not a reactive animal. He is capable of self-determinism. He has willpower. He ordinarily has high analytical ability. He is rational and he is happy and integrated only when he is his own basic personality.

The most desirable state in an individual is complete self-determinism. Such self-determinism may be altered and shaped to some degree by education and environment, but so long as the individual is not aberrated, he is in possession of self-determinism. So long as he is self-determined in his actions he adjusts himself successfully to the degree that his environment

---

2. **pusillanimity:** lacking of courage; cowardliness.

3. **virtues:** ideal qualities in good human conduct.

4. **vices:** evil or wicked actions, habits or characteristics.

5. **dramatizations:** repetitions in action of what has happened to one in experience; replays now of something that happened in the past, out of their time and period.

---

will permit such an adjustment. He will be more forceful, effective and happier in that environment than when aberrated.

That the basic personality is "good" does not mean that he cannot be a terribly effective enemy of those things rationally recognizable as destructive to himself and to his.

The basic individual is not a buried unknown or a different person, but an intensity of all that is best and most able in the person. The basic individual equals the same person minus his pain and dramatizations.

The drive strength of the person does not derive from his aberrations. The aberrations lessen the drive strength. Artistry, personal force, personality, all are residual in the basic personality. This is derived from clinical research and experimentation. The only reason an aberree[6] occasionally holds hard to his aberrations is because his engrams[7] have a content which forbids their removal.

---

6. **aberree:** an aberrated person.

7. **engrams:** moments of pain and "unconsciousness" containing physical pain or painful emotion and all perceptions, and not available to the analytical mind as experience.

5

Engrams

5

Engrams

The reactive mind consists of a collection of experiences received during an unanalytical moment which contain pain and actual or conceived antagonism to the survival of the individual. An engram is a perceptic entity which can be precisely defined. The aggregate of engrams compose the reactive mind.

A new subfield entitled "perceptics" has been originated here to adequately define engramic data. Perceptics contains as one of its facets the field of semantics.[1] Precisely as the field of semantics is organized, so is organized in perceptics each sensory perception.

The audio[2]-syllabic[3] communication system of man has its counterpart in various languages observable in lower animals. Words are sounds in syllabic form delivered with a definite timbre,[4] pitch[5] and volume or sight recognition in each case.

---

1. **semantics:** the scientific study of the meanings and the development of meanings of words.

2. **audio:** of hearing or sound.

3. **syllabic:** having to do with words or portions of words uttered as a single uninterrupted sound.

4. **timbre:** the characteristic or quality of sound that distinguishes one voice or musical instrument from another.

5. **pitch:** that quality of a tone or sound determined by the frequency of vibration of the sound waves reaching the ear: the greater the frequency, the higher the pitch.

Words are a highly specialized form of audio-perceptics. The quality of the sound in uttering the word is nearly as important as the word itself. The written word belongs in part to visio[6]-perceptics. Having but lately acquired his extensive vocabulary, the mind of man is least adjusted to words and their sense. The mind is better able to differentiate amongst qualities of utterance than amongst the meanings of words themselves.

Included in perceptics in the same fashion and on the same axioms as semantics are the other sensory perceptions—organic sensation, the tactile[7] sense, the olfactory[8] sense and the senses involved with sight and hearing. Each has its own grouping. And each carries its class of messages with highly complex meanings. Each one of these divisions of the senses is plotted in time according to the earliest or most forceful significances. Each class of messages is so filed as to lead the individual toward pleasure and away from pain. The classifications and study of this varied sensory file has been designated "perceptics."

Engrams are received into the mind forming a reactive area during moments of lowered analytical awareness of the individual, and they contain physical pain and antagonism to survival. The engram is a packaged perceptic not available to the analytical mind but intimately connected to the physio-animal mind. Under normal conditions it reacts as a dramatization of itself when approximated by the organism's perceptions of its content in the immediate environment during periods of weariness, illness or hypnotic[9] moments in the life of the individual.

---

6. **visio:** the perception of light waves.
7. **tactile:** of, having or related to the sense of touch.
8. **olfactory:** the sense of smell.
9. **hypnotic:** tending to produce sleep or a trance.

When injury or illness supplants[10] the analytical mind producing what is commonly known as "unconsciousness" and when physical pain and antagonism to the survival of the organism are present, an engram is received by the individual. Subsequently, during moments when the potential of the analytical mind is reduced by weariness, illness or similar circumstances, one or more of the perceptics contained in the engram may be observed by the individual in his environment, and without his perceiving that he has observed it (or the identity of it) the individual dramatizes the moment of receipt of the engram.

An engram impedes one or more dynamics of the basic individual. Being antagonistic to his survival it can be considered analogically to consist of a reverse charge.[11]

As an example, the analytical mind can be said to possess multiple scanners in layers. Ordinary, or pleasurable, memory can be considered to have, as an analogy only, a positive charge. The multiple scanners are able to sweep these areas and make available memory data to the analytical mind so that it can arrive by various mathematical means at a solution for its various problems.

The engram, as a specific memory package, can be considered to have a reverse charge which cannot be reached by the scanner of the analytical mind but which is directly connected to the motor controls and other physical functions and which can exert, at a depth not nearly as basic as the basic drive but nevertheless low, a hidden influence upon the analytical mind through another circuit. The analytical mind in awareness of *now*, nevertheless, is unable to discover, without therapeutic

10. **supplants:** takes the place of; supersedes, especially through force or plotting.

11. **charge:** the quantity of electricity or electrical energy in or upon an object or substance.

assistance from an auditor, the existence of such an engram, since it was received during a moment of extremely low potential on the part of the analytical mind.

As a further analogy, and for demonstration only, an engram can be considered to be a bundle of perceptions of a precise nature. An engram is an entire dramatic sequence, implanted[12] during unconsciousness, which possesses specific perceptic keys,[13] any one of which when unanalytically perceived by the individual in his environment, may in greater or lesser degrees set the engram into reaction.

Denied to the analytical mind at its reception, it is denied to the analytical mind in its exact character during its dramatization. Its content is literal and on the physio-animal level, demands action. Man's analytical ability and his vocabulary are imposed above both the physio-animal mind and the reactive mind, both on the evolutionary time track and in awareness. The charge contained in the engram is inexhaustible and remains reactive in full force whenever keyed into the circuit by restimulators.

Restimulators are those approximations in the environment of an individual of the content of an engram. Restimulators can exist in any of the various senses. The orderly filing of perceptics in the memory does not, apparently, include the content of engrams, these being filed separately under an "immediate danger" heading.

There are three kinds of thought: the first is *engramic*, or *literal*. It demands immediate action without examination by the

---

12. **implanted:** planted firmly or deeply, embedded.

13. **keys:** things that secure or control entrance to a place, or provide access to something.

---

analytical mind. A hand being withdrawn from a hot stove when burned is being governed by the reactive principle, but as the ensuing instant of unconsciousness caused by the shock is ordinarily slight, no real engram can be said to have formed.

The second type of thought is *justified thought*. Engramic thought is literal, without reason, irrational. Justified thought is the attempt of the analytical mind to explain the reactive, engramic reactions of the organism in the ordinary course of living. Every engram may cause some form of aberrated conduct on the part of the individual. Justified thought is the effort of the conscious mind to explain away that aberration without admitting, as it cannot do normally, that it has failed the organism.

The third and optimum type of thought is *rational thought*. This is the thought used by a "Clear."

An engram is an apparent surcharge[14] in the mental circuit with certain definite finite content. That charge is not reached or examined by the analytical mind, but that charge is capable of acting as an independent command.

When the basic drive of the individual is boosted in potential by an observed necessity, the residual charge in an engram is insufficient to contest, at times, the raised purpose. The analytical mind can then be seen to function in entire command of the organism without serious modification by engramic command.

At other times, hostility in the environment and confusion of the analytical mind combine to reduce the dynamic potential to such a degree that the engramic command, in comparison to the basic drive, can be seen to be extremely powerful. It is at

---

14. **surcharge:** an additional or excessive load or burden.

---

such times, in the presence of even faint restimulators, that the individual most demonstrates his aberrations.

Example: Engram received at the age of three and a half years. Adult preclear. As child in dental chair, against his will, under antagonistic conditions, given nitrous oxide[15] and tricked by dentist. During painful portion of treatment the dentist says, "He is asleep. He can't hear, feel or see anything. Stay there."

The perceptics which can be restimulated in this are the quality, pitch and volume of the dentist's voice; the sound of the dentist's drill; the slap of the cable running the drill; street noises of a specific kind; the tactile of the mouth being forcibly held open; the smell of the mask; the sound of running water; the smell of nitrous oxide; and in short, several of each perceptic class, excluding only sight.

The effect of this experience, being a part of an engramic chain[16] which contained two earlier experiences, was in some small degree to trance[17] the individual and maintain some portion of him in a regressed[18] state.

This engram is too brief and extraordinarily simple but it will serve as an example to the auditor. The timeless quality of the suggestions, the conceived antagonism, precursors[19] on the engramic chain awakened and reinforced, all these things confused the time sense of the individual and were otherwise reactive in later life.

---

15. **nitrous oxide:** a colorless, nonflammable gas used as an anesthetic and in aerosols.

16. **chain:** a series of incidents of similar types.

17. **trance:** to put in a half-conscious state, seemingly between sleeping and waking, in which ability to function voluntarily may be suspended.

18. **regressed:** gone back; returned; moved backward.

19. **precursors:** earlier engrams.

For every engram there is a somatic[20] as part of that engram. No aberration exists without its somatics unless it is a racial-educational aberration, in which instance it is compatible with its environment and so is not considered irrational.

Every aberration contains its exact command in some engram.

The numbers of engrams per individual are relatively few. The aberrated condition of the individual does not depend on the number of engrams but the severity of individual engrams.

An engram is severe in the exact ratio that it is conceived by the organism to have been a moment of threat to survival. The character of the threat and the perceptic content produce the aberration. A number of engrams with similar perceptics in an individual produce a complex aberration pattern which nevertheless has for its parts individual engrams.

An aberration is the manifestation of an engram and is serious only when it influences the competence of the individual in his environment.

Engrams are of two types depending upon the duration of restimulation. There are *floaters* and *chronics*. A floater has not been restimulated in the individual during the lifetime succeeding it. A chronic is an engram which has been more or less continuously restimulated so that it has become an apparent portion of the individual. A chronic begins to gather "locks."[21] A

---

20. **somatic:** body sensation, illness or pain or discomfort. *Soma* means body.

21. **locks:** analytical moments in which the perceptics of the engram are approximated, thus restimulating the engram or bringing it into action, the present-time perceptics being erroneously interpreted by the reactive mind to mean that the same condition which produced physical pain once before is now again at hand.

---

floater has not accumulated locks since it has never been restimulated.

A lock can be conceived to be joined to an engram in such a way that it can be reached by the multiple scanners of the analytical mind which cannot reach the engram. A lock is a painful mental experience. It is or is not regarded by the analytical mind as a source of difficulty or aberration. It is a period of mental anguish and is wholly dependent upon an engram for its pain value. When an engram is activated into a chronic, it accumulates numerous locks along the time track of the individual. The engram itself is not immediately locatable, except somatically, along the time track of the individual. Locks are of some diagnostic[22] value but, as they exist as experiences more or less recallable by the analytical mind, they can be depended upon to vanish upon the removal of the engram from the reactive mind, without further auditing.

The running of a lock as a lock has some therapeutic value but the exhaustion[23] of locks from an aberrated individual is long and arduous and is seldom productive of any lasting result. Upon the location and exhaustion of the engram from the reactive mind, all of its locks vanish. An engram may exist unactivated as a floater for any number of years or for the entire duration of an individual's life. At any future moment after the receipt of an engram, whether that time period consists of days or decades, the floater may reactivate into a lock at which time it becomes part of the commands obeyed by the analytical mind in its efforts to rationalize. The removal of the individual from his restimulators, which is to say, the environment in which the engram was reactive, is in itself a form of therapy, since the

22. **diagnostic:** of or constituting a careful examination and analysis of the facts in an attempt to understand or explain something.

23. **exhaustion:** the act of drawing out or draining off completely.

engram may then return to its status as a floater. But such a return will not remove the locks, which the analytical mind can then recall as painful experiences.

Example: *Engram*—At birth occurs the phrase "no good," uttered during a moment of headache and gasping on the part of a child.

Lock: At the age of seven while the child was ill with a minor malady,[24] the mother in a fit of rage said that he was "no good."

The removal of the engram also removes, ordinarily, without further attention, the lock.

Note: Birth remained inactive in the above case as a floater until the moment of reduced analytical power at the age of seven when a birth phrase was repeated. It is worth remarking that the entire content of the birth engram is given simultaneously both to the child and to the mother, with only the difference of somatics. It is further worthy of note that the mother quite often perceives in the child a restimulator and uses against it the phrases which were said when the child gave the mother the greatest pain, namely, birth. The child is then victimized into various psychosomatic ills by the repetition of its birth engram restimulators, which may develop even more seriously into actual disease.

The mind controls the multiple and complex functions of the growth and condition of the organism. Containing organic sensation as one of its perceptics, the engram then, when reactivated, causes a somatic and additionally may deny body fluids, i.e., hormones[25] and blood, to some portion of the anatomy,

---

24. **malady:** a disease, illness or sickness (used figuratively).

25. **hormones:** substances formed in some organ of the body (glands) and carried by a body fluid to another organ or tissue, where it has a specific effect.

occasioning psychosomatic ills. The denial of fluid or adequate blood supply may result in a potentially infective area. The psychosomatic reduces the resistance of some portion of the body to actual disease.

Somatic and other sensory errors find their basis in unconscious antagonistic moments. A somatic may be adjusted by an address to a lock but the permanency of adjustment obtains[26] only until such time as the engram is again reactivated, causing another lock.

All aberrations are occasioned by engrams.

An engram is severely painful or severely threatening to the survival of the organism and is an engram only if it cannot be reached by the awake analytical mind.

A simple approximation of the action of an engram can be accomplished by an experiment in hypnotism whereby a positive suggestion[27] which contains a posthypnotic[28] signal is delivered to an amnesia[29]-tranced person. The subject, having been commanded to forget the suggestion when awake, will then perform the act. This suggestion is then actually a light portion of the reactive mind. It is literally interpreted, unquestionably followed, since it is received during a period of unawareness by the

---

26. **obtains:** is in force or in effect; prevails.

27. **positive suggestion:** suggestion by the operator to a hypnotized subject with the sole end of creating a changed mental condition in the subject by implantation of the suggestion alone. It is the transplantation of something in the hypnotist's mind into the patient's mind. The patient is then to believe it and take it as part of himself.

28. **posthypnotic:** of, having to do with or carried out in the period following a hypnotic trance.

29. **amnesia:** partial or total loss of memory caused by brain injury or by shock, repression, etc.

analytical mind or some portion of it. The restimulator, which may be the act of the operator adjusting his tie, causes the subject to commit some act. The subject will then try to explain why he is doing what he is doing, no matter how illogical that action may be. The posthypnotic suggestion is then recalled to the subject's mind and he remembers it. The compulsion vanishes (unless it is laid upon an actual engram).

The obedience of the subject to the command has, as its source, engramic thought. The explanation by the subject for his own action is the analytical mind observing the organism, which it supposes to have in its sole charge, and justifying itself. The release of the posthypnotic suggestion into the analytical mind brings about rational thought.

Engrams can be considered to be painfully inflicted, often timeless, posthypnotic suggestions delivered antagonistically to the "unconscious" subject. The posthypnotic suggestion given the subject in the above example would not have any permanent effect on the subject even if it were not removed by the operator, because there was presumed to be no antagonism involved (unless, of course, it rested on a former engram).

The physio-animal mind of an organism never ceases recording on some level. The exact moment when recording begins in an organism has not at this date been accurately determined. It has been found to be very early, probably earlier than four months after conception and five months before birth. In the presence of pain, any moment prior to the age of two years may be considered to be unanalytical. Any painful experience received by the fetus[30] contains its full perceptic package, including darkness.

---

30. **fetus:** in man, the offspring in the womb from the end of the third month of pregnancy until birth.

Once an auditor has worked a prenatal[31] engram and has seen its influence upon the engramic chain and the awake life of the adult, no question will remain in his mind concerning the actuality of the experience. That the fetus does record is attributable to a phenomenon of the extension of perceptions during moments of pain and the absence of the analytical mind.

Laboratory experiment demonstrates that under hypnosis an individual's sensory perception may be artificially extended.

The existence of pain in any large degree is sufficient to extend the hearing of the fetus so that it records, during the existence of pain and the presence of exterior sound, the entire and complete record of the experience. As a chronic engram is but precariously[32] fixed on the mind, the syllables or voice timbres contained in the prenatal will reactivate the somatic and the emotional engramic content whenever the approximations of that engram appear in the child's (or the adult's) vicinity.

The understanding of language is not necessary to reactivate an engram since the recording of the brain is so precise that the utterance of the identical words in similar tones during later prenatal periods or during birth, or immediately after birth, can and may occasion the original prenatal or any of the prenatals to become reactive, producing locks, injuring the health of the infant or, for that matter, of the fetus.

The perceptics of the fetus are extended only during moments of pain. But a chain of prenatal engrams can occasion a condition wherein the hearing of the fetus is chronically extended, forming numerous locks before birth. These locks will

---

31. **prenatal:** existing or taking place before birth.

32. **precariously:** in a manner dependent on chance circumstances, unknown conditions or uncertain developments; uncertainly.

vanish when the actual engrams are discovered and exhausted from the psyche.

Any painful unanalytical moment containing antagonism is not only a matter of record but a source of potential action in the human organism at any period during its lifetime, reserving, of course, the question of when the fetus first begins to record.

Birth is ordinarily a severely painful unconscious experience. It is ordinarily an engram of some magnitude. Anyone who has been born then possesses at least one engram. Any period of absence of analytical power during receipt of physical pain has some engramic potentiality.

Moments when the analytical power is present in some quantity, when physical pain is absent and only antagonism to the organism is present do not form engrams and are *not* responsible for the aberration of the individual.

Sociological maladjustments;[33] parental punishments of a minor sort, even when they include pain; libidos;[34] childhood struggles and jealousies are not capable of aberrating the individual. These can influence the personality and environmental adjustment of the individual but so long as he is not pathologically[35] incompetent, he can and will resolve these problems and remain without aberration.

The human mind is an enormously powerful organism and its analytical ability is great. It is not overlaid above naturally unsocial or evil desires, but is founded upon powerful and

---

33. **maladjustments:** examples of lack of harmony between the individual and his environment.

34. **libidos:** sexual urges or instincts.

35. **pathologically:** in a manner due to or involving disease.

---

constructive basics which only powerful, painful and antagonistic experiences can impede. Engrams will be found to have been conceived by the individual as intensely antagonistic to the survival of the organism.

The discovery of the basic[36] engram is the first problem of the auditor. It normally results in an engramic chain. The content of that chain will be found to be physically severe.

An engram is physically painful; is conceived by the organism as an antagonistic threat to its survival; and is received during the absence of the analytical power of the mind. These factors may vary within the engram so that an engram may be of minimal pain, maximal antagonism and minimal absence of the analytical power, but no engram is available to the scanners of the consciousness.

Note: One has as much functioning analyzer as one has awareness of *now.*

The body is to some degree reliving the experience of the engram whenever the experience is restimulated. A chronic psychosomatic, such as a painful arm, indicates the chronic, continuous coexistence with *now* of the moment the arm was broken or hurt. Several engrams reactivated into a chronic state bring several moments of unconsciousness, pain and antagonism into a coexistence with *now.* The engram is a bundle of perceptics which include, as the primary manifestation, organic sensation. The organic sensation is enforced on the members of the body to a greater or lesser degree whenever, and as long as, the engram is restimulated. There is only *one* psychosomatic command which is common to all engrams. Any engram contains this as

36. **basic:** the earliest engram on an engram chain.

part of the command it will enforce upon the body. The analytical mind is an organism and a part of the human body. As a stomach may be made to ache chronically (ulcers), to feel broken, the engram also enforces a command upon the *organ* of the analytical mind. That command is common to every engram. Engrams are valid only when they are received during a momentary dispersal or shocked, null condition of the analytical mind.

Every engram contains and enforces the command on the analytical mind that *it has been dispersed and is not operating.* This is common to every engram. This is reduction of the intellect by engrams totally aside from specific engramic content. It explains at once insanity and the remarkable mental facility of a cleared individual.

6

Aberrations

6

Aberrations

All aberrations of any kind are of precisely the same nature (as covered in the last chapter). It is the content of the engram which causes the aberration and forms its nature. Complexity amongst engramic contents may demonstrate a most complex aberration.

The various commands contained in the engrams, reactivating and modifying the basic dynamic command of the mind, produce abnormal characteristics in the behavior of the analytical mind which are chronic or sporadic[1] as the engrams occasioning them are restimulated. An entire concept of existence may be built from engramic content. Conflicts in the commands contained in engrams and conflicts between the basic drive and the engramic contents combine into behavior patterns.

When the organism has become so impeded that it can no longer influence or command its environment, it can be considered to be insane in that environment. Change of environment may relieve the condition or, more certainly, the exhaustion of the content of the reactive mind will restore the ability of the

---

1. **sporadic:** happening from time to time; not constant or regular; occasional.

analytical mind to solve the problems with which it is confronted.

Whatever the engramic content of the reactive mind and its potential influence upon the behavior of the individual, it does not necessarily follow that the reactive mind may be chronically restimulated. However, when the reactive mind has been restimulated consistently, the analytical mind, called upon to solve the problems around and through antagonistic and incorrect data, may be unable to perform its task. In the absence of disease or injury, any mind not in a physiological amnesia state may be restored to normal function by the removal of the reactive mind. It should be noted however that this is modified by the fact that patients who have received insulin shocks,[2] prefrontal lobotomies,[3] electric shocks and other shock treatments are regarded as equivocal[4] and are temporarily classed with disease cases for lack of adequate observation in this stage of the experimental research.

People can be regarded as rational or irrational only insofar as they react in their customary environment. But any person in possession of a reactive mind is an unknown quantity until that reactive mind has been examined. If he has been examined his mind can be cleared in the same process.

There are several factors contained in the engrams in the reactive mind which most certainly tend toward aberration. These include engramic commands which derange the time sense of the individual and thus apparently destroy his time

---

2. **insulin shocks:** states of collapse caused by a decrease in blood sugar resulting from the administration of excessive insulin.

3. **prefrontal lobotomies:** operations on the prefrontal lobes of the brain.

4. **equivocal:** suspicious; questionable.

track, and engrams which contain restimulators of such time-lessness and such perceptic content that they remain thereafter continually with the individual and seem to arrest him or regress him in time. Engrams containing commands which make the individual chronically unable to conceive differences are especially harmful since these tend to compare everything to engramic value and thus cause the individual to arrive at a chronic state of engramic thinking.

The mind resolves problems related to survival, utilizing its ability to conceive similarities and observe differences.

Engrams which destroy or tend to hold in suspension the analytical mind's ability to conceive associations most influence the apparent intelligence of the mind. But engrams which tend, by their command content, to destroy the mind's ability to conceive differences may produce severe aberration.

Example: "All men are alike," received as powerful engramic content would tend to compare and associate every man with those men contained in the reactive mind as painful and dangerous.

An aberration may attain any form or complexion.[5] As a rough analogy: A compulsion may be conceived to be an engramic command that the organism *must* do something; a repression is a command that the organism must *not* do something; a neurosis is an emotional state containing conflicts and emotional data inhibiting the abilities or welfare of the individual; and a psychosis is a conflict of commands which seriously reduce the individual's ability to solve his problems in his environment to a point where he cannot adjust some vital phase of his environmental needs.

---

5. **complexion:** general appearance or nature; character; aspect.

All this variety of manifestation of aberration is occasioned by the pain-enforced commands or contents of engrams.

Physical aberrations are occasioned by engrams when they are not the result of injury or disease; even then, the aspect may be improved by the exhaustion of the reactive mind of the sick individual. The engram cannot manifest itself as a mental aberration without also manifesting itself to some degree as somatic aberration. Removal of the somatic content of engrams, which is also necessary to obtain any other relief, may occasion glandular readjustment, cellular growth, cellular inhibition and other physiological corrections.

7

The Tone Scale

7

The Tone Scale[1]

The Tone Scale denotes numerically, first, the status of an engram in the reactive mind, next, its erasure[2] or reduction, and provides a measure for sanity in an individual.

The derivation of this scale is clinical and is based upon observation of engrams being worked. When an engram is located and developed,[3] the extreme range it can follow begins with apathy, develops into anger (or the various facets of antagonism), proceeds into boredom and arrives at last in cheerfulness or vanishes utterly.

The Tone Scale is essentially an assignation of numerical value by which individuals can be numerically classified. It is not arbitrary but will be found to approximate some actual governing law in nature.

---

1. **Tone Scale:** the scale of emotional states which range from death at the bottom, up through apathy, grief, fear, covert hostility, anger, antagonism, boredom, conservatism, cheerfulness, to enthusiasm at the top.

2. **erasure:** the action of going over and describing the content of an engram until it has vanished entirely.

3. **developed:** made known or apparent; disclosed.

Zero is equivalent to death. An individual with a zero tone would be dead.

Ranging upwards from 0 to 1 is then that emotional bracket which may be denoted as apathy along its graduated scale from death to the beginnings of apathetic resentment.

From 1 to 2 is the range of antagonism, including suspicion, resentment and anger.

Boredom and its equivalents, by which is denoted minor annoyance, begins at 2 and ends at 3.

From 3 to 4 are the emotions which range from carelessness to cheerfulness.

The term *tone* 4 denotes a person who has achieved complete rationality and cheerfulness.

Each engram residual in the reactive mind has its own independent tonal value. Serious engrams will be found in the apathy range. Dangerous engrams will be found in the anger range. Above 2.5 an engram could not be considered to have any great power to affect the analytical mind. Each engram in the reactive mind then can be said to possess a tone value. The composite sum of these engrams will give, if added, a numerical value to the reactive mind.

Engrams can be computed as they lie along the dynamics, and to each dynamic may be assigned a tone. The sum of the tones of the dynamics, divided by the number of the dynamics will give a potential numerical value for an individual. This, of course, is variable depending on the existence of restimulators in his environment to reactivate the engrams. The general tone of an individual is important both in diagnosis and in establishing a resolution to the case.

The probable average of mankind at this writing may be in the vicinity of 3.0. Complete rationality depends upon exhaustion of the reactive mind and complete rationality is invariably the result of reaching tone 4.

The initial diagnosis is done by the assignation of a general tone to denote the condition of an individual's reactive mind.

His methods of meeting life, his emotional reaction to the problems in his environment, can be evaluated by the use of the Tone Scale.

In auditing, as will be covered later, an engram normally can be expected to run from its initial value in the apathy or anger range to tone 4. Very shortly after it reaches tone 4 it should vanish. If it vanishes without attaining the laughter of tone 4 it can be assumed that the individual's basic engram has not been erased.

The Tone Scale has value in auditing and should be thoroughly understood.

8

The Character of Engrams

8

The Character
of Engrams

There are several general types of engrams. It must be understood that the mind possesses a time track of one sort or another and that this track is a specific thing. The time track of an individual will include all those things available to his analytical mind when in a light trance or during regression.[1] However, a person can be regressed and the data which he can easily contact along his time track is definitely not engramic even if it possesses an emotional charge. Everything on this track will be rational or justified experience. It will not include engrams. It may include locks—which is to say, that it may include moments of mental anguish or antagonism and may even include instants of unconsciousness which have some slight engramic command value.

An engram has several specific, positive characteristics. It is received by the individual at some moment of physical pain. It is not available to the analyzer and it includes conceived or actual antagonism to the survival of the organism. Certain mechanisms such as "forget it" may swerve a minimumly painful or unconscious experience off the time track. In that case it becomes possessed of engramic command value.

---

1. **regression:** a technique by which part of the individual's self remained in the present and part went back to the past.

All engrams with power to derange the analytical mind and aberrate the physical body lie off the time track and are not available to the analytical mind.

By reason of its disorganization during the moment the engram was received, or because it has been forcibly instructed that the data in the engram is not to be recalled, the analyzer cannot reach the engram by ordinary means because the data has been erroneously labeled "dangerous," "important" or "too painful to touch." The engram then, by a bypass circuit, feeds hidden commands into the analyzer. By a direct instantaneous circuit it is permanently connected to the motor controls, all perceptic channels, the glands and heart. It is awaiting a moment of low general tone, weariness or injury when the analytical mind has reduced powers. It is also awaiting the perception of one or more of the engram's restimulators in the environment of the organism.

Continuous restimulation of the engrams can, in itself, cause a low general tone which in its turn permits more engrams to become restimulated. As the reactive mind comes into a more or less completely chronic state of reaction, the individual becomes more and more governed by this mind. His thought becomes more and more engramic and he can be seen to drop in general tone on the Tone Scale down to the break point which may be arbitrarily placed somewhere between 2 and 2.5 and below which lies the region of insanity.

Engramic thought is irrational, identity thought by which the mind is made to conceive identities where only vague similarities may exist. It is necessary that the auditor thoroughly understand engramic thought, for it is with this complete irrationality of identity that he will basically deal. As he works with any preclear, sane or insane, he must continually employ in the bulk of his computation on the case the equation of engramic thinking.

Engramic thinking can be stated by: A equals A equals A equals A equals A.

The engram, when one or more of its restimulators is perceived in the environment during a moment of low general tone, may dramatize. The dramatization *is* the precise content of the engram. The aberration is the precise content of the engram. The reaction of an individual's analytical mind when an engram is reactivated is justification.

There is reason to believe that part of this survival mechanism consists of the axiom: **The analyzer must never permit an incorrect solution.** The engram brings about many incorrect solutions. The analyzer may very well become entirely involved with the attempt to discover and deliver to a society, or to itself, adequate rational reasons for the behavior of the organism.

The analytical mind, though working from the command of the engram itself, is unaware of the source of the command. Not being able to discover the source, it introverts[2] more and more in an effort to solve a problem which contains danger to the organism. The analytical mind tends to find the danger without and within the organism.

There are five ways that the organism can react to a danger in its vicinity. It can attack it, avoid it, neglect it, run from it or succumb[3] to it. In just these ways can the analytical mind, which, it must be remembered, *is* possessed of self-determinism and willpower, react to the reactive mind. As the general tone lowers, which is to say, as the analytical mind becomes less and less powerful through weariness, continual reverses[4] in general

2. **introverts:** directs (one's interest, mind or attention) upon oneself.

3. **succumb:** to give way (to); yield; submit.

4. **reverses:** changes from good fortune to bad; defeats.

health, etc., the more and more heed it must give to the problems unsolved in the reactive mind. These are in essence unsolved problems. As such, they contain their own solutions. The analytical mind, unable to reach them, justifies the organism's reaction to them (succumbs to them), causes the organism to attempt to flee from them, apathetically may neglect them (as in prefrontal lobotomy), avoids them in many intricate ways or attacks them. The analytical mind is not only not certain where the experience lies on the time track, it also does not know whether the menace is within the organism or without it. So, it can become entirely indiscriminate[5] and eventually it may achieve highly irrational solutions by which it seeks to solve the problems of the highly irrational reactive mind.

The deep sensory perception channel entering the mind is evidently equipped with an "appreciator" which sorts according to the momentary general tone or potential of the analytical mind. The higher the general tone or potential of the analytical mind the better the data in the appreciator is sorted. The appreciator circuits are evidently fully apprised[6] of engramic content in the reactive mind and evaluate restimulators perceived in the environment against the general tone of the analytical mind. When that is low, restimulators route more or less directly to the reactive mind which instantly responds by fixed connections into the motor controls. Commands to the various members, muscles, glands and organs of the body may be sporadic or constant, producing a high variety of responses in the body. Entire vocabularies are fed into the voice circuits directly from the reactive mind when an engram is restimulated. Orders to be active or inactive are fed to other portions. The individual time track of the engram spaces the commands to the organism and a

---

5. **indiscriminate:** not recognizing the differences between; not making careful choices or distinctions.

6. **apprised:** informed or notified.

---

dramatization is accomplished which may contain a portion or all of the content of the engram as governed by the situation. Psychosomatic ills, hysterias,[7] rages, tantrums,[8] criminal acts and any and all content prejudicial[9] to the survival of the organism in which the organism is seen to be indulging has as its source the reactive mind.

The sole and only content of the reactive mind is *what exterior sources have done TO the organism.*

None of the content of the reactive mind is self-motivated. The auditor is then interested only in what is done *to* the person, not what the person himself has done, since, for purposes of auditing, the acts of the organism in its society can be discounted[10] beyond diagnosis. Even then they are of small importance to the auditor.

An organism possessed of an analytical mind, not victimized by incapacitating disease or injury and unimpeded[11] will commit no act knowingly prejudicial to the survival of the organism or other factors within the dynamics. It will combat only those dangers in society which are actual menaces.

Whatever may be the status of the "innate[12] moral sense," the basic intent of the basic personality is to further various

7. **hysterias:** outbreaks of wild, uncontrolled excitement or feeling, such as fits of laughing and crying.

8. **tantrums:** violent, willful outbursts of annoyance, rage, etc.; childish fits of bad temper.

9. **prejudicial:** tending to injure or impair.

10. **discounted:** disregarded partly or wholly.

11. **unimpeded:** not possessed of engrams.

12. **innate:** existing naturally rather than acquired; that seems to have been in one from birth.

energy forms along the dynamics toward the goal. Only moments of actual dispersal of the awareness of the analytical mind permit data to be received which is prejudicial to the intent of the dynamics. Only from these "unconscious" moments can the basically stable and enormously powerful and able analytical mind be aberrated through the implantation of unanalyzed, painfully administered and antagonistic information. It is the purpose of the auditor to find and exhaust these moments from the life of the individual. Dianetic auditing includes therefore, as its basic principle, the exhaustion of all the painfully unconscious moments of a subject's life. By eradicating pain from the life of an individual, the auditor returns the individual to complete rationality and sanity.

The auditor should never be content with merely bringing the person back to normal. He should achieve with the person a tone 4 even though this is far in advance of the average state of society at this time. A tone 4 with his drives intact and powerful, with his rationality and intelligence increased to the optimum, becomes extremely valuable to the society, whatever his past.

Knowing this the auditor can expect a maximum result of lasting duration with any preclear not physically hopeless.

A Dianetic auditor will achieve the best results by ignoring impulses to educate or inform the subject in any way beyond instructions sufficient to acquire cooperation.

The entire purpose of the auditor is to rehabilitate the basic dynamic and the normal purpose or profession of the individual whom he audits. Anything implanted by positive suggestion or "education" in the course of auditing is harmful and must be cancelled if delivered. Only the basic personality of the individual can decide and evaluate things in his environment. Therefore, hypnotism as practiced with positive suggestions should be shunned since any and all hypnotic commands with the attendant forgetter[13] mechanisms are no more than artificially implanted engrams. Indeed, it is quite usual for the auditor to have to exhaust hypnotically implanted material received either from some hypnotist or from the analytical mind itself when the person has been operating under auto-control.[14] Hypnotism as such does not work, and a study and short practice in Dianetics will reveal exactly why.

The auditor is attempting to delete the reactive mind from the individual. This reactive mind is an infestation of foreign, careless and unreasoning commands which disrupt the self-determinism of the individual to such an extent that he no longer has charge, through his analytical mind, of the organism itself, but finds himself under the continual and chronic orders of unseen, never-reviewed exterior forces, often and usually antipathetic to the survival of the organism.

Engrams deal with identities where no identities exist. They therefore pose many strange and irrational problems which are seen as aberrations in preclears. If a human being has been born, he can be supposed to have at least one engram. Anyone who has a birth which has not been cleared by auditing has therefore a reactive mind. There is no disgrace attached to having a reactive mind since it was thrust without his consent and without his knowledge upon an unconscious and helpless individual. Sometimes this was done by persons with the best of imaginable intentions. A person not possessed of a rational mind cannot be rationally considered to be morally responsible, no matter the

13. **forgetter:** any engram command which makes the individual believe he can't remember.

14. **auto-control:** autohypnosis or an attempt to process oneself without an auditor. If attempted in Dianetics, autohypnosis is probably as close to fruitless masochism as one can get. If a patient places himself in autohypnosis and regresses himself in an effort to reach illness or birth or prenatals, the only thing he will get is ill.

demands of the current society which hitherto lacked any method of determining responsibility.

The pain contained in the reactive mind is normally severe. The usual parental punishments, family complications, reprimands, minor accidents and the battle of the individual with his environment influence, but do not cause, a reactive mind, nor do these things have the power to change materially the reactions of an individual.

In the background of any individual exist many hidden personalities contained in the reactive mind. Dealing in identities, the reactive mind often confuses identities of individuals. Therefore, irrational attachments and antipathies are formed by aberrated individuals who can often find no reason for such attachments or antipathies in their contemporary[15] environment.

The content of an engram is literally interpreted, not as it was stated to the "unconscious" subject, but as it was received in its most literal phraseology[16] and perception.

The organism possesses many inherent mechanisms and abilities by which it can learn or preserve or forward itself along the dynamics. Any one of them may be exaggerated by engrams to a point where it becomes an actual threat to the organism or impedes it. Engrams can and do aberrate all the sensory perceptions, any and all parts of the body and the mind itself. By demanding suicide the engram can destroy the entire organism.

The error of the reactive mind was introduced by the evolution of speech, for which the basic mechanism was not designed. When all perceptics save speech formed the reactive mind, it was

15. **contemporary:** up-to-date.
16. **phraseology:** choice and pattern of words; way of speaking or writing.

to some degree serviceable. With speech came such complexities of perception and such interchanges of ideas that a whole series of illusions[17] and delusions[18] could be derived from the reactive mind's necessity to determine identities for purposes of emergency.

Without the reactive-type mind, survival would be extremely difficult, since it must be there to care for emergencies during moments of dispersal of the analytical mind by shock or other means.

With speech the reactive mind came to possess far more power and extensive content. The analytical mind, being a delicate mechanism in some respects no matter how rugged and capable in others, then could become subjected to delusions and illusions which, however shadowy and unreal, must nevertheless be obeyed. By stripping the reactive mind of its past painful content the analytical mind may be placed in complete command of the organism.

The moment a man or a group becomes possessed of this ability, it becomes possessed of self-determinism. So long as these possess reactive minds, irrationalities will persist. Because it contains literal speech, no reactive mind can be conceived to be of any value whatsoever to the rational organism since the methods of that reactive mind remain intact and will continue to act to preserve the organism in times of "unconsciousness" of the analytical mind. There is no residual good in any reactive mind. It is capable of any illusion. It has no assist power along the dynamics save only to cancel or modify other reactive mind content. The source of the individual's power and purpose is not

---

17. **illusions:** false perceptions, conceptions or interpretations of what one sees.

18. **delusions:** beliefs in things that are contrary to fact or reality, resulting from deception, misconception or mental disorder.

derived from the reactive mind but from the basic dynamic and its eight divisions. Any auditor will establish this to his own satisfaction after he has run a very few cases.

When an individual during auditing is attempting to "hold on to his aberrations," the auditor may be assured that that person has as part of the content of the reactive mind such phrases as, "don't dare get rid of it," which, identically translated, apparently applies to aberrations. It may, in fact, apply in an engram containing an attempted abortion.

The identity factor in the reactive mind may cause the analytical mind to respond irrationally in auditing and to justify the aberrations in many irrational ways. Whatever means he uses or statements he makes to avoid the exhaustion of his reactive mind is contained exactly in the reactive mind as a positive suggestion and has no application whatsoever in rational thought.

Individuality (if by that is meant a man's desires and habits) is not traced to the reactive mind save when by individuality is meant those flagrant[19] eccentricities[20] which pass in Dickens[21] for characters.

A man is much more an individual after his reactive mind has been cleared.

---

19. **flagrant:** very bad and obvious.

20. **eccentricities:** deviations from what is ordinary or customary, as in conduct or manner; oddities; unconventionalities.

21. **Dickens, Charles:** (1812–70) English novelist of the late 19th century whose books are noted for picturesque and extravagant characters in the lower economic strata of England at that time.

9

Dramatization

9

Dramatization

Dramatization is the duplication of an engramic content, entire or in part, by an aberree in his present-time environment. Aberrated conduct is entirely dramatization. Aberrated conduct will occur only when and if an engram exists in the reactive mind of the aberree. That conduct will be a duplication of such an engram. The degree of dramatization is in direct ratio to the degree of restimulation of the engrams causing it. A mild dramatization would be a similarity to the engram. A severe dramatization would be an identity with the engram.

The general tone of an aberree, when high—when his person is unwearied and he is well and not directly menaced in his environment—does not permit as great an influence by the reactive mind, since the tone level of the entire individual possesses too great a differential[1] from the tone level of the engram, which is always low on the Tone Scale. As the general tone of the individual approaches the tone level of the engram under restimulation, dramatization becomes more severe.

The analytical mind is present to the degree that the general tone of the aberree is high. As this general tone lowers through

1. **differential:** a difference between comparable things.

ill health, reverses or constant restimulation of the reactive mind, the analytical mind is proportionately less aware. Dramatization is demonstrated by the aberree in inverse ratio to the potential of the analytical mind. A geometrical progression[2] is entered as general tone lowers to cause the analytical mind to lose its entire awareness potential. Since every engram contains, as the common denominator of all engrams, the unconsciousness of the organ which is the analytical mind, dramatizations gain rapidly as this interaction progresses.

In the presence of a relatively high analytical mind awareness potential, dramatization takes the form of similarity. The data of the engram is present but is interspersed[3] with or modified by justified thought. The physical pain which is always present as part of the dramatization is equally mild, a duplication of the pain which was present during the engram. The awareness potential of the analytical mind reduces in the restimulation of the engram which again reduces the general tone.

The aberree is subject to almost continuous dramatization of one engram or another as the restimulators appear in his vicinity. (Although the aberration may be so mild as to include only some chronically affected organ.) Complete dramatization is complete identity. It is the engram in full force in present time with the aberree taking one or more parts of the dramatis personae[4] present in the engram. He may dramatize all the actors or merely one of them. His dramatization is identity, is unreasoned and always entirely reactive. When the analytical mind reaches the low point of awareness potential it held during the

---

2. **geometrical progression:** progression with a constant ratio between successive quantities, as 1:3:9:27:81.

3. **interspersed:** scattered among other things; put here and there or at intervals.

4. **dramatis personae:** the characters in a play or story (used here to refer to people present in the engrams of the aberree).

engramic incident, that point is also forced upon the aberree as a part of the dramatization. The aberree may also dramatize himself as he was at the moment of the engram's receipt.

The words, physical actions, expressions and emotions of an aberree undergoing an identity dramatization are those of the single or various dramatis personae present in the engram.

An engram which can be dramatized may at any time in an aberree's future be dramatized as an identity dramatization when and if his general tone is low and his environment becomes infiltrated by restimulators.

An aberree, because of high general tone and other factors, may not suffer the restimulation of an engram for a number of years after its receipt. A large number of engrams may be present and undramatized in any aberree, if he has never been presented with their particular restimulators in an optimum moment for restimulation. The common denominator of all insanity is the absence of all or almost all awareness potential in the analytical mind. Insanity can be acute[5] or chronic. Any identity dramatization is insanity, by which is meant the entire absence of rationality.

The aberree commonly and chronically dramatizes locks. The engramic content may compel or repress the aberree whenever restimulated.

An irrational person is irrational to the degree that he dramatizes or succumbs to engramic content in his reactive mind. The computations which can be made on the basis of dramatization are infinite. The reactive mind thinks in identities.

---

5. **acute:** severe, but of short duration.

Dramatizations are severe as they approach identity with the engrams which force them into being in the conduct of the aberree.

The Dianeticist can profit in many ways by these principles of dramatization. By examination of the rage or apathy or hysteria patterns of the preclear, the Dianeticist will find himself in possession of the exact character of the engrams for which he is searching.

In the case of the manic,[6] the fanatic or the zealot, an engram has entirely blocked at least one of the purpose lines deriving from a dynamic. The engram may be called an "assist engram." Its own surcharge (not the dynamic force) leads the individual to believe that he has a high purpose which will permit him to escape pain. This "purpose" is a false purpose not ordinarily sympathetic[7] with the organism, having a hectic[8] quality derived from the pain which is part of it, even though that pain is not wittingly experienced. This "assist engram" is using the native ability of the organism to accomplish its false "purpose" and brings about a furious and destructive effort on the part of the individual who, without this "assist engram" could have better accomplished the same goal. The worst feature of the "assist engram" is that the effort it commands is engramic dramatization of a particular sort, and if the engram itself is restimulated the individual becomes subject to the physical pain and fear which the entire experience contained. Therefore, the false purpose itself is subject to sporadic "sag."[9] This sag becomes

---

6. **manic:** a person whose life force is channeled straight through an engram and whose behavior, no matter how enthusiastic or euphoric, is actually highly aberrated.

7. **sympathetic:** showing favor, approval or agreement.

8. **hectic:** characterized by confusion, rush, excitement, etc.

9. **sag:** loss of firmness, strength or intensity; weakening through weariness, age, etc.

---

longer and longer in duration between periods of false thrust. It is easy to confuse, in casual observation, an "assist engram" and an actual, valid drive, unless one also observes the interspersed periods of "sag." The "assist engram" may or may not occasionally accomplish something, but it does accomplish a confusion in the society that the dynamics of the individual are derived from his bad experiences. This is a thing which is emphatically[10] untrue.

Inherently the individual has great willpower. This however can be aberrated. Willpower or its absence occasions the attitude of the aberree toward his reactive mind.

The prevention of the dramatization of an engram or a lock further reduces the dynamic thrust of the aberree. Chronic prevention lowers his general tone toward the break point. Unhampered dramatization, as it contains restimulation of a physical pain and the reduced potential of the analytical mind, produces other harmful effects.

Necessity can and does render inactive the entire reactive mind.

Dramatization occurs most often in the absence of necessity or when the reactive mind has obscured the presence of necessity.

Dramatization is residual in the motor controls including speech and can be allayed[11] by the physical exhaustion of the individual. The organism during dramatization tends to revivify[12] toward the moment of the engram's occurrence; the engram

---

10. **emphatically:** decidedly; decisively.

11. **allayed:** lessened, relieved or alleviated.

12. **revivify:** to relive an incident or some portion of it as if it were happening now.

containing, as one of its identity parts, the complete physical condition of the organism as at the moment of laying-in of the engram.

There is no folly or facet of human activity which cannot be dramatized. An immediate alleviation can be achieved when addressing an aberree who is in identity dramatization by acting upon the fact that the conditions of auditing, with one exception, already exist, i.e., a reduced potential in the analytical mind and the preclear returned[13] to the moment of occurrence. Affinity may be established and Dianetic auditing begun at once. He can be persuaded to listen for the phrases he is uttering and they can be alleviated by exhaustion on routine procedure.

13. **returned:** the person has "sent" a portion of his mind to a past period on either a mental or combined mental and physical basis and can reexperience incidents which have taken place in his past in the same fashion and with the same sensations as before.

10

The Auditor's Code

10

The Auditor's Code

$\mathbf{N}$ot because it is a pleasant thing to do or because it is a noble[1] idea, the auditor must always treat a preclear in a certain definite way which can be outlined as the Auditor's Code. Failure to follow this code will cause trouble to the auditor, will considerably lengthen and disturb his work and may endanger the preclear.

The auditor in the first place, at the optimum, should be himself cleared; otherwise he will find that many of his own engrams are restimulated as he listens to the engrams of his preclears. This restimulation may cause his own engrams to become chronic, victimizing him with various allergies[2] and delusions and causing him to be, at best, extremely uncomfortable.

An auditor can audit while he himself is being cleared as this is a peculiar and special method of locating his own engrams, since they become restimulated. Becoming painful to him, they can be found and speedily removed.

---

1. **noble:** very good or excellent; superior of its kind.

2. **allergies:** conditions of excessive sensitivity to specific substances such as foods, pollens, dust, etc., or conditions (as heat or cold) which in similar amounts are harmless to most people; they are manifested in physiological disorders.

Even if he is not himself cleared, the auditor must act like a Clear towards the preclear. The Auditor's Code is the natural activity of a Clear.

The auditor must act toward the preclear exactly in the way that the preclear as an organism would desire that his own conscious analytical mind would react to and consider the organism.

An affinity must therefore be maintained at all costs. The auditor must never permit himself to lose his temper, become aggravated, to scold or badger or antagonize the preclear in any way. To do so would not merely disturb the comfort of the preclear but might additionally derange him and might even prohibit further beneficial therapy by the auditor.

The code is nearly "Christlike."

The auditor must be confident in that he must continually reassure the preclear when restimulated engrams cause despondency[3] on the preclear's part. A cheerful optimistic presence encourages the preclear through his most painful experiences.

The auditor must be courageous, never permitting himself to be intimidated[4] by either the aggression or hostility of the preclear.

The auditor must be kind, never indulging in hostilities or personal prejudices. The auditor must be trustworthy, never

---

3. **despondency:** loss of courage or hope; dejection.
4. **intimidated:** made timid or afraid.

betraying or capriciously[5] denying a preclear and above all never breaking his word to the preclear. An auditor must be clean for personal odors or bad breath may be restimulators to the preclear or may disturb him. The auditor must take care not to offend the concepts or sensibilities of the preclear.

The auditor must be persistent, never permitting the case of the preclear to either resist him or to remain unsolved until it is in a proper tone 4, since the restimulation of engrams is a malady unto itself unless they are being properly exhausted.

The auditor must be patient, never hurrying or harassing the preclear beyond the needs of stirring an engram into view. He must be willing to work at any and all times necessary and for the length of time necessary to exhaust the engrams in process of elimination.

In addition to these things it may be remarked that a definite affinity is established between the auditor and preclear during the time of auditing. In the case of opposite sexes this affinity may amount to an infatuation.[6] The auditor must remain aware of this and know that he can and should redirect the infatuation to some person or activity other than himself when auditing is at end. Not to do so is to produce an eventual situation wherein the preclear may have to be rebuffed[7] with consequent trouble for the auditor.

---

5. **capriciously:** in a manner characterized by or subject to whim; impulsively or unpredictably.

6. **infatuation:** the condition of being inspired with foolish or shallow love or affection.

7. **rebuffed:** bluntly or abruptly rejected, as of a person's advances.

11

Auditing

11

Auditing

The auditing technique consists of assisting the preclear's analytical mind or some part of it with the auditor's analytical mind. The auditor then functions during each successive period of auditing, and only during the periods themselves, as an extra analytical mind of the preclear.

The reactive mind was received during the dispersal or inactivity of the analytical mind. The reactive mind is removed by "returning" the preclear to the engram, and laying its contents before the scrutiny[1] of the analytical mind.

This technique may be considered the lowest common denominator of a number of techniques. *Anything* which will serve this purpose and permit auditing to be accomplished efficiently is valid technique.

The optimum is purely personal affinity brought about by understanding communication with the preclear on agreeable subjects. Another and almost useless method is narcosynthesis[2] together with the various drugs and hypnotics used to produce

---

1. **scrutiny:** a close examination; minute inspection.
2. **narcosynthesis:** drug hypnotism.

sleep. Methods can be found such as faith healing, books on medical hypnosis, the techniques of Indian medicine men and so forth. It is pointless to delineate these methods here. They are currently available under the name of hypnotism but a caution should be enjoined[3] that hypnosis as itself is not at all acceptable to Dianetics and indeed has extremely limited use. Briefly, however, it must be remarked that if hypnotism is studied to advance these techniques, all positive suggestion and posthypnotic suggestion must be avoided as these suggestions depend for their effectiveness upon the already existing content of the reactive mind and will only form additional locks.

Any and all so-called hypnotic drugs have definite drawbacks since they, like so many other things, may be termed "shotgun" methods. These paralyze not only the analytical mind but the remainder of the organism so that it is nearly impossible to obtain the proper somatic reaction in the preclear. They are not hypnotics but anesthetics. By using them the auditor instantly denies himself the main material which will lead him to the engram, which is to say, restimulated physical pain. Such restimulated pain is never of very great magnitude and is obliterated by the use of anesthetics.

At no time should the auditor permit the preclear to be under the delusion that he is being treated by hypnosis. This is mentioned because hypnotism is a current fad and the principles of Dianetics have nothing whatever to do with hypnotism. Both are based upon simple natural laws but have between them an enormous gulf. One is the tool of the charlatan[4] and the other is the science of the human mind.

Regression in its simplest form, hereafter called *return*, is

3. **enjoined:** urged or imposed with authority; ordered; enforced.
4. **charlatan:** a person who pretends to knowledge or skill; quack.

employed in Dianetic auditing. It would be an extraordinary case which required revivification. Return is the method of retaining the body and the awareness of the subject in present time while he is told to go back to a certain incident. Dates are not mentioned. His size is not mentioned. Various means are used to restimulate his memory. Any of the perceptics may be employed to return him to some period of his past. He is told simply to "go back to the time when——." He is asked to recount what he can of the incident. He is told that he is "right there" and that he can "recall this." Little else is said by the auditor save those hints necessary to return the preclear to the proper time.

The preclear is not allowed at any moment to revivify in that period since the data is drained as a surcharge from his time track to present time. He is told that he can remember this, but he is never told that he can remember this in present time since that will occasion the somatics to return to present time. Most of the data is located by observing some somatic pain in the individual or some somatic aberration and seeking to discover wherein it was received.

The somatics are employed primarily because the motor controls possess a less disturbed time track than the sensory strip.[5] Anything which tends to lighten these somatics is then antipathetic to auditing. It must be remembered that there is no aberration without an accompanying somatic. The somatics alone, being physical ills of one sort or another, hold the aberrated content of the reactive mind in place. The motor controls can be returned to a period although the conscious or analytical mind believes itself to be entirely in present time. By talking to the muscles or motor controls or various bodily aches and pains, the auditor can shift them at will up and down their time track.

---

5. **sensory strip:** the sequential physical record of pain or discomfort of any kind from conception to present time.

This time track is not connected to the analytical mind and speech, but is apparently a parallel time track with greater reliability than the sensory track. The precision of data contained in the motor control time track is enormous. Muscles can be made to tense or relax. Coughs, aches and pains can be made to come and go simply by uttering the right words for the engrams, or the wrong words.

It is the primary task of the auditor to cause the time tracks of the motor strip and the sensory strip to come into parallel. That the time track exists in the strips has not been proven but they can so be considered for the purposes of this explanation. That they exist is extremely apparent. The motor strip time track can be asked questions down to the smallest moment of time, and the area of an engram can be so located and its character determined.

As an analogy, a dream may be considered as the reception by the remaining analytical mind of a distortedly reflected and indirectly received picture of the engrams. This applies only when the dream is specifically directed at the reactive mind. It will be found that a preclear with a large and active reactive mind does not dream to any great extent in normal sleep but that a Clear may dream pleasantly and consistently. A dream in its normal function is that powerful and original mechanism called the imagination, compositing or creating new pictures.

The use of the dream is not highly technical and has little value in Dianetics. The auditor gleans[6] data from the preclear by his own remarks about any subject or by the preclear's illogicalness on a subject. The auditor tells the preclear to dream about this data. When the preclear has had the dream he is directed to

---

6. **gleans:** collects or gathers anything little by little or slowly.

go back to the engram causing the dream. Quite often he will do so. If he does not, or if he becomes hostile, it is certain that an engram exists on the subject.

The lie detector, the encephalograph[7] and many other means are of limited usefulness in determining both the character and the extent of the engrams since into these as into the dreams can be fed the restimulators of the preclear. A codified restimulator list can be created which will be found to be common to most preclears. It should include all types of illnesses, accidents, the common trite[8] phrases of the society and names of various persons who commonly surround a child during his childhood. Such a codified restimulator list would be interesting for experiment and every auditor can compose his own. These are best composed after auditing the individual preclear and after inquiry into his life to determine the various irrationalities of thought.

In that engrams are identity thought, the remarks of the preclear about his engrams will be found to be included in the content of those engrams. When the preclear is asked to imagine a bad situation at certain ages and under hypothetical conditions, he will very often deliver up a complete engram. The auditor must realize that every remark that a preclear makes while he is going over his reactive mind is probably some part of the content of that reactive mind. That mind is literal. The words the preclear uses when referring to it must be literally evaluated.

---

7. **encephalograph:** an instrument for measuring and recording the electric activity of the brain.

8. **trite:** worn out by constant use; no longer having freshness, originality or novelty; stale.

12

Diagnosis

12

Diagnosis

It is a useful and positive principle that whatever confronts or contests the analytical mind of the preclear will also confront and contest the analytical mind of the auditor. When the auditor is acting as the analytical mind of the preclear, whatever emotion or antagonism is directed toward him is the emotion or antagonism which is directed by the reactive mind toward the preclear's own analytical mind. If a preclear cannot hear what people are saying in his engrams, he has another engram about "can't hear." If he cannot feel anything in his engram, it is because he has an engram about "can't feel." If he cannot see, he has an engram about not being able to see, and so forth. If he cannot return, he has an engram about going back or returning to childhood or some such thing. If he is doubtful and skeptical about what is happening or what has happened to him, it is because he has an engram about being doubtful and skeptical. If he is antagonistic, his reactive mind contains a great deal of antagonism. If he is self-conscious or embarrassed, it is because his reactive mind contains self-consciousness or embarrassment. If he insists on maintaining his own control, refusing to do what the auditor tells him to do (although he is returned), it is because he has an engram about self-control, and so forth and so on. This is identity thought and is used in diagnosis.

The return is the best method of learning the problems of the preclear. Trying to work the preclear into remembrance, hearing, seeing, feeling, going back and forward, going to sleep, awakening and taking due note of what he says about the entire process will form a rather complete diagnosis on one who is not insane. Questioning the preclear as to what is wrong with him while returned will elicit[1] replies straight out of his principal engrams. Listening to an endless justification of his actions is both a delay and a waste of time, but listening to what he has to say about what he thinks has happened to him or what he is afraid of is of definite value.

Insane preclears form and pose a slightly different but essentially the same problem.

It is a clinically established observation that the reactive mind is relatively shallow. Below it lies the basic personality of the individual no matter how "insane" he may be. Therefore, by one means or another, a rational being may be reached within a preclear, a being which is not aberrated. It is this fact of non-aberration which makes the basic personality a difficult aid in diagnosis. Here however it can be established what the preclear really wants, what he hopes, what he actually feels. It has been observed that no matter what his raving[2] state, providing his brain structure is normal and complete, the basic personality is entirely sound and sane and will cooperate. After auditing, the preclear will become this strong, competent and able personality.

The reactive mind, when unable to exert itself to its aberrated full in the environment of the person, will break the person or cause him to lose tone. Therefore it is of definite interest to

---

1. **elicit:** to draw out (information, a response, etc.).

2. **raving:** talking wildly or furiously, talking nonsensically in delirium; *raving mad,* completely mad.

discover what immediately preceded the break of the preclear or what is currently causing him unhappiness. Something is dispersing his dynamics. The probability is that he has a chronic restimulator in his vicinity. Wives, husbands, mothers, fathers, superiors, etc., can be the source of such breaking since they turn the purpose of the reactive mind, which pretends to desire above all else the best interest of the person, back upon the person himself. Thus these sources cause the individual to lower back into the tone of the reactive mind (apathy or a low tone 2).

The problem of the fixed person and the problem of the sympathy engram are both visible in the aberrated individual. The identity thought of the reactive mind has taken some part of the personality of some individual in the current environment and referred it to some part of the personality of an individual in the engramic past. The discovery of this identity is one of the principal problems of auditing. The sympathy engram is of a very specific nature, being the effort of the parent or guardian to be kind to a child who is severely hurt. If that parent or guardian has shown the child antagonism prior to the time of the injury, the adult (preclear) is prone to reactivate the injury in the presence of the identity personality with whom he is now associated. This causes many somatic ills to present themselves in the present. Only the exact words of a sympathy engram will soothe the aberrated personality.

There are not many personality types. A human being learns through mimicry. If his own self is found to be too painful he can become another self and very often does. A tone four can become another person at will without being aberrated about it, thus enjoying books and plays by "being" the person portrayed. But an aberrated individual can become part of the engramic cast of his reactive mind and so solve all of his problems in such an aberrated fashion. Aberrated persons are not themselves since they do not possess their own determinism.

As has been stated, those emotions, doubts, worries and problems which confront the auditor when attempting to place the preclear in reverie[3] or to work him in that reverie will lead the auditor into the basic content of the reactive mind.

There are certain definite manifestations which can be suspected and certain routines which follow every case. Every human being has been carried in the womb and every human being has been born. The discovery of the basic engram on each chain is extremely necessary for the commencement of auditing. Finding the basic engram is like taking the enemy in the flank.[4] There is nothing before it, therefore the end most remote from the adult life of the individual is the end most exposed for the attack of the auditor.

In the basic engram the preclear can see, feel, hear and freely emote.[5] When he is returned to later incidents, it may be found that he cannot do these things no matter how hard the auditor works to enable him to do so. By pursuing the engramic chain up its chronological sequence, this ability will be restored. Therefore it is necessary first and foremost to locate the basic engram. This may, in some few cases, lie later than birth. In the majority of the cases it will be found to lie at or before birth. No discussion is here entered about the ability of the human mind to remember at such remote periods. It can be stated however that when engramic data does exist, the time track is opened by pain and antagonism at these extreme points and can be contacted and exhausted. It is with the greatest difficulty that the auditor will find the basic engram. Since it is ordinarily quite painful, and the scanning mechanism hasty as its purpose (or one of its

---

3. **reverie:** a light state of "concentration" not to be confused with hypnosis; in reverie the person is fully aware of what is taking place.

4. **flank:** the right or left side of a body of troops, etc.

5. **emote:** to give expression to emotion.

purposes) is the avoidance of pain, it will not easily reach them. Like the scanning mechanism on a cathode ray tube,[6] the scanners of even a very reduced potential analytical mind sweep over, skipping and not touching the data on the engramic chain. By various means the auditor must then require the scanners to contact that data and force the data back onto the time track where it can be properly exhausted.

Light prenatals are the best possible approach to a case. When the only prenatal is an extremely heavy one or an attempted abortion (which, by the way, are very common), the auditor must use a great deal of guile.[7] Dream therapy, causing the patient to imagine and other mechanisms are sometimes useful in discovering the basic engram. It can be said that the basic engram and the beginning of the actual engram chains is very early, before, near or during birth, is painful, and will not be easily contacted. In that few preclears have more than a few hundred serious engrams, the task is light when once begun but requires a great deal of imagination and persuasion.

A prenatal must always be suspected unless birth, when lifted,[8] rises easily into a tone 4. If none of the engrams will rise into a tone 4, the auditor would suppose that he has not discovered the basic. There are three kinds of engrams: the precursor, the engram and the follower. By engram here is meant that experience which the auditor has found and is working upon. If it does not seem to be lifting after a few recountings, a precursor (earlier engram) must be suspected and returned to. In this way

---

6. **cathode ray tube:** a vacuum tube, for example, a television picture tube, in which beams of electrons are directed against a fluorescent screen where they produce a luminous image.

7. **guile:** slyness and cunning in dealing with others; craftiness.

8. **lifted:** raised and vanished; dispelled.

an earlier basic may be discovered. Blows in the womb, attempted abortions and birth are the usual basics. Easily the most important are the prenatals.

When a child is abnormally afraid of the dark, he probably has a severe engramic experience in prenatal. This prenatal experience will include all the sound data and sensory data of the incident. It is eidetic[9] and identical. The preclear will have somatics. These on the first few recountings will be ordinarily faint and then become more severe as more data is located. The data will finally be in a more or less complete state and the engram will begin to lift, rising up through the various tones. All prenatals are apathy experiences and are therefore serious.

Minor taps and discomforts in the womb are of no consequence. A true engram will consist of such a thing as a knitting needle being rammed through the fetus, half of the fetus' head being badly injured, blows of various kinds bringing about fetal unconsciousness and so forth. Return eventually will find an opening into any period when there has been pain.

Disbeliefs and antagonisms from the preclear on the subject of such a thing as an attempted abortion should be overlooked by the auditor or taken into account as the sign of an existing engram. A case is recalled wherein a girl insisted that if an abortion had ever been attempted on her it should have been successful. Through several sessions, while an attempt was made to lift birth, she continued this assertion until the auditor realized that this was probably a remark made by the abortionist (or the mother) when his efforts failed. As soon as this was suggested to the girl she was able to contact the actual incident. A

---

9. **eidetic:** designating or of mental images that are unusually vivid and almost photographically exact.

chronic apathy case under treatment for some years in an institution, she suddenly responded to auditing, brought the abortion to tone 4, erased birth to tone 4 and recovered mentally and physically into a social asset well above normal.

The auditor should continue to suspect prenatals so long as he cannot get later engrams easily into tone 4. Once an engramic chain has been lifted at its end nearest to conception, the preclear should begin to clear relatively automatically, aided but little by the auditor. The erasure should be in terms of laughter at its optimum. This laughter is the reversing of charges residual in the locks which depended for their fear content or antagonistic content upon the basic engrams.

Abortion attempts are easy to recognize when an auditor has had some experience. The parent who attempted the abortion will, after birth, likely be a source of anxiety to the individual who seems to require a great deal of affection and attraction from that parent. The individual will be found to be most fond of the parent (or other) who did not aid, or who actually tried to prevent the abortion attempt. At this time abortion attempts are extremely common.

When an abortion attempt has been lifted, the engramic chain should easily be brought to the time track and exhausted.

Auditing is essentially very simple but it demands precise understanding of the principles involved and imagination and sympathy on the part of the auditor. He must learn to compute engramically—or learn to think with his analytical mind, only for the purposes of auditing others, engramically. His biggest problem is the discovery of the basic of basics. It may elude him for a considerable period of time.

There is, however, preparatory work to do in a case other

than the discovery of the basic. Occasionally an entire time track must be rehabilitated in which "do not remember" and "can't remember" have obscured the track. Later locks can be found and exhausted in the same manner that engrams are exhausted, and rapid scanning methods may be developed in the future for these. The hysteria or fear of the individual can be momentarily allayed one way or the other and the problem of reaching the basic can be entered upon. There are as many types of cases as there are cases, but these are the primary fundamentals.

An auditor must think his way through every case, taking as his data the constantly reiterated[10] statements of the preclear during auditing, and accumulating experience as to how incidents can be thrust off the time track, burying them from sight of the analytical mind, thus forming a reactive mind to the detriment[11] of the organism.

---

10. **reiterated:** repeated (something done or said); said or done again or repeatedly.
11. **detriment:** loss, damage, disadvantage or injury.

13

Exhaustion of Engrams

13

Exhaustion
of Engrams

The technique of exhausting an engram is not complicated but it must be adhered to. An engram is an unconscious moment containing physical pain and conceived or actual antagonism to the organism. Therefore, that engram before it is discovered will exhibit antagonism toward the auditor trying to discover it. When it is first discovered, it may be found to be lacking in its essential data. There are many techniques by which this data can be developed. In a prenatal engram the analytical mind apparently must redevelop the situation. Many returns through the incident are therefore necessary.

When an engram will not exhaust, the first thing the auditor should suspect is an earlier engram. It is actually possible for a later one to contain essential information which will not permit the information to rise. In the course of auditing, when an engram is restimulated by the auditor but will not rise above apathy and does not seem to contain all the necessary data, the auditor must look for an earlier engram, and it almost inevitably will be found to exist. This precursor is then developed as the basic engram. If it follows the same behavior pattern of not lifting or becoming complete, another previous to it must be discovered. If at last the auditor is entirely certain that there is no engram ahead of the one being run, some possible locking mechanism later on may be found and exhausted, at which time the basic may show itself. Continual application of energy to the basic will at length bring it into full view and continual recountings of it will gradually develop it, raise its tone and lift it into tone 4.

The principle of recounting is very simple. The preclear is merely told to go back to the beginning and to tell it all over again. He does this many times. As he does it the engram should lift in tone on each recounting. It may lose some of its data and gain other. If the preclear is recounting in the same words time after time, it is certain that he is playing a memory record of what he has told you before. He must then be sent immediately back to the actual engram and the somatics of it restimulated. He will then be found to somewhat vary his story. He must be returned to the consciousness of somatics continually until these are fully developed, begin to lighten and are then gone. Tone 4 will appear shortly afterwards. If the preclear is bored with the incident and refuses to go on with it, there is either an earlier engram or there is other data in the engram which has not been located.

The auditor will discover that an engram, occasionally when lifted into a 3, or even erased, without reaching laughter, will sag. This is a certain sign of an earlier basic on that chain. Any kind of sag from a tone 4 is impossible if tone 4 has truly been reached. Tone 4 will not be reached if there are earlier basics. The engram may vanish and be erased, but there will be no cheerfulness or laughter about it at the end if it is not the basic.

Once the basic has been reached and brought into tone 4, it will disappear. The next engram on the chain will be located and rather easily brought into tone 4. If one is accidentally skipped, the third in line will be found to hold or sag. The intermediate must then be located and brought into a tone 4. In such a way the chain will gradually come up into a complete tone 4. At this time the locks, the merely mentally painful incidents in the person's life, will begin to clear automatically. These will erase or lift without any attention from the auditor. While these are clearing, the auditor must concern himself with secondary engrams.[1] These would be engrams on their own if they had not had forerunners. They therefore do not relieve after the removal of the basic but must be located as themselves. These in turn will start a chain of releasing locks which again need no attention. There may be entirely distinct engramic chains in the reactive mind which are not appended in any way to the original basic.

So long as a preclear retains any part of a reactive mind, he will be interested in himself (in the condition of his mind) and introverted. Therefore, so long as he is interested in his own reactive mind, he is impeded in his dynamic pursuit of survival. A guarantee of a tone 4 is the patient's interest in positive action along his dynamics and his application of himself to the world around him. Introversion is not natural nor is it necessary to the creation of anything. It is a manifestation of the analytical mind trying to solve problems on improper data, and observing the organism being engaged in activities which are not conducive to survival along the dynamics. When a Clear has been reached, the basic personality and self-determinism of the individual will have asserted itself. No somatics chronic in the present will remain (excepting those which can be accounted for by actual disease, injury or malconstruction of the brain).

Though more germane[2] to Child Dianetics, it is of help to the auditor to know that a child can be considered to have

---

1. **secondary engrams:** engrams which are engrams of the same character and kind and on the same drive line as the basic engram of a chain. An engram chain is then composed of a basic engram and a series of secondary engrams.

2. **germane:** truly relevant; pertinent; to the point.

formed his general basic purpose in life somewhere around the age of two. This purpose is fairly reliable, as at that time his engrams have probably not gained much force over him since his responsibilities are slight. He will have tried to hold his main purpose throughout his life but it will undoubtedly have been warped both by his reactive mind's experience content and by his environment. The time when the purpose is formed varies and may indeed never have manifested, as in the case of amentias.[3] As the preclear is normally interested in this purpose and its rehabilitation, he will often take a more intense interest in auditing if there is an attempt made to discover it. This purpose is quite valid and the preclear can be expected to rehabilitate his life along its dictates[4] unless he is too oppressed by his environment. (It can be remarked that a Clear will ordinarily order or change his environment.)

Vocational[5] therapies have as their source the tenet[6] of the rehabilitation of the general purpose of an individual or the establishment of a false purpose in order to allay the activity of his reactive mind. It has little bearing on Dianetics and more properly belongs in Medical Dianetics, but an auditor, for the term of auditing, may engage his preclear along the purpose line of becoming a Clear. This is not necessary and is indeed often automatic since the basic personality beholds at last a chance to manifest itself. However, it will occasionally aid the auditor.

The auditor should be prepared to have to solve many individual problems since above these basics are almost as many

---

3. **amentias:** conditions of feeblemindedness or mental deficiency.

4. **dictates:** guiding principles or requirements.

5. **vocational:** designating or of education, training, etc., intended to prepare one for an occupation, sometimes specifically in a trade.

6. **tenet:** a principle or belief held as a truth, as by some group.

problems as there are cases. For example, in the case of a preclear who has several very nasty prenatals it will be found that the formation of the body in the womb has overlaid or confused the time track so that a later prenatal must be partially lifted before an earlier prenatal can be exhausted. This is often true of a later period of life. In one case an entire series of prenatals was held down by a dental operation under nitrous oxide at the age of twenty-five. Until some portion of this was removed, the bulk of the prenatals were not available. In short, the circuits of the mind can become entangled to a point where even the motor control time track is confused.

Dispersal of purpose by some engram along some dynamic or purpose line is a common situation and is indeed the basic concept. As a stream of electrons[7] would behave if they were to encounter a solid object in their path, so does a drive or purpose disperse. These many varied and faint tracks after impact with the engram are symptomatic. Along dynamic two, the sexual drive, promiscuity[8] inevitably and invariably indicates a sexual engram of great magnitude. Once that engram is removed promiscuity can be expected to cease.

Anxiety is established in the preclear's mind by such dispersals and he dramatizes because of the dispersal. This is one of the manifestations of his malady. No pervert ever became a pervert without having been educated or abused by a pervert. And that abuse must have been very thorough.

The contagion[9] of engrams is an interesting manifestation which the auditor should and must observe. It can be said that

---

7. **electrons:** particles of matter with a negative electric charge.
8. **promiscuity:** having casual, random sexual relations.
9. **contagion:** communication or transfer from one to another.

insanity runs in families, not because this is a eugenic[10] truth but because a standard patter[11] during emergencies or stress creates certain types of engrams which in turn create types of insanities. Insanities are so definitely contagious that when a child is raised by aberrated parents, the child becomes aberrated. As would be delineated by Child Dianetics, the best way to guarantee a sane child is to provide it with cleared parents. This is of definite interest to the auditor since he will discover that in cases of severe prenatals and birth the engrams were also received by the mother exactly as they were received by the child. The child will thereafter be a restimulator to the mother and the mother a restimulator to the child for the severe incidents. The mother, having received the exact wording of the engram, also contains the engram. Restimulation by the child will occasion the use of the engramic language toward the child. This brings the infant and child and adolescent into the unhappy situation of having his birth engram or his prenatal engrams continually restimulated. This occasions dire[12] results and very great unhappiness in the home and is one of the main sources of family difficulties.

A child, even if he despises them, will dramatize the actions of his parents when he himself is married and when he himself has children. In addition to this the other partner in the marriage also has his or her own engrams. Their engrams combine into doubled engrams in the children. The result of this is a contagion and a progression of aberration. Thus any society which does not have a high purpose finds itself declining and gaining to itself greater numbers of insane. The contagion of aberration is at work progressively and the children become progressively aberrated until at last the society itself is aberrated.

---

10. **eugenic:** pertaining or adapted to the production of fine offspring especially in the human race.

11. **patter:** the talk of a group or class.

12. **dire:** dreadful; terrible.

While the fate of society belongs definitely in Social and Political Dianetics, the auditor is interested in the fact that he can take the prenatal and birth content of the engrams of his preclear and run them to discover postbirth locks and secondary engrams. The mother will normally have used much the same data whenever the troubles of the child impinged upon her reactive mind; this of course accounts for the locks.

The auditor will also discover that where he has a married preclear who is aberrated, he should have two preclears, which is to say, the partner. It is useless to return a preclear to his or her aberrated spouse and expect domestic tranquility to result. While the Clear cannot and will not pick up his old engrams from the spouse in whom he has implanted them, he will, nevertheless, find his life made unbearable by the mere existence of a spouse that he himself may have aberrated.

Further, the children of these people will also need auditing, since they will be found (if the parents' aberrations were of any magnitude) to be sickly or aberrated or deficient in some way. The auditor should therefore, when he undertakes a case, be prepared to assume the family of his preclear, should an investigation of that preclear make it seem necessary.

Aberrations are contagious and where a person has been aberrated, his environment will to some degree also have become aberrated. The preclear may, for one thing, be somewhat victimized and impeded by his reactive mind which is now existing in his associates.

The auditor should not permit such terms as *psychoneurotic*,[13] *crazy* or *mentally exhausted* to exist for long in the preclear's

---

13. **psychoneurotic:** neurotic: a person who is mainly harmful to himself by reason of his aberrations, but not to the point of suicide.

mind. These are depressive and are actually aberrations in the society. It is true and provable that the preclear is on his way to being, not a person who is crazy or neurotic, but an individual who will have more stability and self-command and ability, possibly, than those around him. To be blunt: This is not the process of reviving corpses into a semblance of life. It is a process which, at its best usage, is taking the "normal" and "average" and giving them their birthright of happiness and creative attainment in the world of man.

14

Engram Chains

14

Engram Chains

More than one engramic chain will be found in every aberree. When this person becomes a preclear the Dianeticist does well to discover the earliest chain. It is not always possible to do this with accuracy since a preclear is sometimes in such a nervous condition that he cannot be worked on his basic chain but must be alleviated in a greater or lesser degree by the exhaustion of a later and more available chain. This last, however, is not the usual case.

The Dianeticist should clearly understand certain working principles and definitions. By an engram is meant a moment of unconsciousness accompanied by physical pain and conceived antagonism. There are two classes of engrams. One is the basic engram which is the earliest engram on an engram chain. The other is the secondary engram which is an engram of the same character and kind on the same drive line as the basic engram of the chain. An engram chain is, then, composed of a basic engram and a series of secondary engrams. Engram chains also contain locks which are instances of mental anguish more or less known to the analytical mind. These are often mistaken by the preclear for the cause of his conduct. A true engram is unknown to the conscious computer of the preclear but underlies it as a false datum on which are erected almost equally unknown secondaries and an enormous number of locks.

In order to release an engram chain it is vital and absolutely necessary to discover the engrams of that chain. An individual will have more than one engram chain but he has a basic chain. This must be cleared as soon as possible after auditing is engaged on the preclear.

When an engram is discovered by the Dianeticist, he must examine the aspect of it to determine whether or not it is the basic. Discovering it is not, he must immediately determine an earlier basic, and so forth until he is obviously on the scene of the basic engram.

There are certain tests which he can apply. A basic engram will rise to laughter, "sag" slightly, and then rise to tone 4 and vanish. Successive engrams will then erase from that chain with very little work. Almost any engram on an engram chain can be exhausted, but if it is a secondary and not a basic engram it will recede and vanish at times but will rise in part again when the basic engram has been reached and the preclear is brought forward into its area.

A secondary is subject to "sag." Which is to say, that it may be brought to the two point zero (2.0) tone, but after a certain length of time has elapsed—from one to two days—it will be found to have "sagged" and to be, for instance, in a one point one (1.1) tone. It can be successively lifted until it is apparently in a three point zero (3.0) tone, at which point much of its content will disappear. This is reduction.

Any engram chain can be reduced to some degree without reaching the basic but when the basic has been reached, the basic itself and subsequent secondaries can be brought rapidly to tone 4 providing no secondaries are skipped on the return up the time track.

When an engram chain has been brought to tone 4, it can be

considered to have vanished although, while the preclear can no longer find it on the time track (he may even be unable to recall some of its most painful and disheartening aspects), the mind apparently has been proofed against the data it has contained. A search for an engram chain after it has been exhausted and a tone 4 has been achieved should, for purposes of auditing, be entirely fruitless.

Once the basic has been discovered and the engram chain has been brought to tone 4 the locks will vanish of their own accord. If this does not occur then there is something remaining or the auditor has been too optimistic about the selection of his basic engram for the chain and has not, in reality, discovered it.

All engram chains should be exhausted from a preclear. These may be discovered to lie along the various dynamics but any chain may influence more than one dynamic.

Another type of engram is the cross engram. This is usually a childhood or adult engram which embraces more than one engram chain. The receipt of the cross engram, containing as it does the convergence of two or more engram chains, is often accompanied by a "nervous breakdown" or the sudden insanity of an individual. A cross engram may occur in a severe accident, in prolonged or severe illness under antagonistic circumstances or a nitrous oxide operation. Cross engrams are very easy to locate but should not be addressed by the Dianeticist as such, since an enormous amount of work upon them will not exhaust them until the basics and the chains on which the cross engram depends have been brought to tone 4.

Postbattle neurasthenia[1] is almost always traceable to the

---

1. **neurasthenia:** a type of neurosis characterized by irritability, fatigue, weakness, anxiety and, often, localized pains or distress without apparent physical causes: formerly thought to result from weakness or exhaustion of the nervous system.

---

receipt of a cross engram. This must be, of course, an engram in its own right, as well as a secondary on more than one chain. It is conceivable that a secondary may be so severe that it "breaks" the individual even if it lies on only one chain.

There are certain rules the Dianeticist may employ to establish the basic engram of a chain. In first entering a case these rules apply as well to the first goal which is the location of the basic engram of the basic chain.

Number one: No engram will lift if the basic of that chain has not been lifted.

Number two: The basic engram will not lift until the basic instant of the basic engram has been reached, which is to say, the first moment of the engram. Ordinarily this is the most obscure.

Number three: If after two or three test recountings of an engram it does not seem to be improving, the auditor should attempt to discover an earlier engram.

Number four: No engram is valid unless accompanied by somatic pain. This may be mild. Incidents which do not contain somatics are either not basics (the pain either having been suspended by some such command as "can't feel" in the basic) or else they may not even be engrams.

Cases should be entered as near as possible to the basic engram. Then they should be returned to earlier incidents until the basic is discovered.

The running of locks themselves may accomplish some alleviation of a case.

15

Prenatal, Birth and Infant Engrams

15

Prenatal, Birth and Infant Engrams

The human mind and the human anatomy are enormously more powerful and resilient[1] than has commonly been supposed. Only incidents of the greatest magnitude in physical pain and hostile content are sufficient to aberrate a mind.

The ability of the mind to store data can scarcely be over-rated. In early life before sound is analyzed as speech a human being receives and stores exact impressions of everything which occurs. At some future date, when similar perceptics are encountered, the reactive mind reanalyzes—on the basis of identities only—the content of the early mind. This becomes the foundation of the postconception personality. The actual personality in the individual is powerful and very difficult to aberrate. Unlike animals, which can be driven mad by minor mechanisms of experimental psychology,[2] a man must be most severely handled before he begins to show any signs of derangement. That derangement proceeds from the ability of the reactive mind to store perceptions from the earliest moments of existence and retain

---

1. **resilient:** recovering readily from illness, depression, adversity or the like.

2. **psychology:** the study of the human brain and stimulus-response mechanisms. Its code word was "Man, to be happy, must adjust to his environment." In other words, man, to be happy, must be a total effect.

them on either the analytical or the reactive plane for future reference.

The basic personality does not proceed from engrams and the dynamics of the individual are impeded, not enhanced, by engrams. The dynamics are entirely separate and are as native to the individual as his basic personality, of which they are a part.

Information falls into two categories: the educational or experience level, banked and available to the analytical mind on at least its deeper levels; and aberrational, or data stored in the reactive mind and often used by but never reached by the analytical mind, save through auditing.

There would seem to be two types of recording. The first is cellular recording in which the cells would seem to store data. In that cells in procreating become themselves again—which is to say that when cell A divides, both halves are still cell A—cellular intelligence is not lost. Personal identity is duplicated. In the case of individual men, procreation is far more complex and individual identity is lost—the son is not the father but a genetic[3] composite of vast numbers of ancestors.

The cells of the human being shortly after conception are capable of enormous perceptic and retentive power. After a very short time in the womb, the brain and nervous system are already operating. From then until birth the human being is apparently capable of computations of a rather complex nature on the analytical mind level. Far more certainly he retains information on the reactive level.

Fear, pain and unconsciousness extend the range of perception of the individual. When the human being in the womb is

---

3. **genetic:** pertaining to the line of father and mother to child, grown child to new child and so forth.

injured his senses extend so as to record sounds outside the mother's body. He records them so well that their precise nature is stored for future reference. The human being in the womb responds exactly as it does after birth to the receipt of engrams, storing the data with precision and reacting to it.

The repair facilities available to a human being before birth are greatly enhanced by the presence of ample connective tissue,[4] oxygen and sustenance.[5] These repair facilities are unimaginably great so that a prenatal human being can be severely torn and ripped without becoming structurally deficient. It does, however, receive engrams and these are subject to restimulation. In many cases of attempted abortions it was found that large sections of the prenatal human being's brain could apparently be injured without the brain being deficient or even scarred after birth. These repair facilities do not however lessen the extreme severity of the engrams which can be received by the prenatal human being. The word *fetus* is dropped at this point and it is advised that it should be dropped from the language as a description of a prebirth human being. Insufficient evidence is at hand to make an outright declaration that attempted abortions are responsible for the bulk of our criminal and insane aberrees. But according to the cases at hand the attempted abortion must be accounted responsible for the majority.

The attempted abortion is the most serious aberration producer. So exact is the recording of the prebirth human being, or prenatal, that the reactive mind makes no errors in recognizing its enemies after birth. The mind becomes aberrated in having to depend upon these same enemies for the ordinary sustenance of life while the child is a helpless infant.

---

4. **connective tissue:** tissue found throughout the body, serving to bind together and support other tissues and organs.

5. **sustenance:** food itself, nourishment.

The diagnosis of a prenatal case is relatively simple. Nearly all preclears will be found to have at least one prenatal engram and the case will not solve unless that prenatal is reached and exhausted.

The Dianeticist can usually establish the attempted abortion preclear by an investigation of the conduct of the infant and child. Uneasiness or unhappiness in the home, a feeling of not being wanted, unreasonable fear and a strong attachment to grandparents or another nonparental member of the household are often signs of an attempted abortion. Fear of the dark is usually but not always a part of the attempted abortion case. The auditor should suspect an abortion attempt in every preclear he audits, at least for this next generation. Whether or not the preclear disbelieves the diagnosis is of no importance to the auditor as the prenatal engrams may very well contain the words "can't believe it." The parents themselves, as well as society, mislead the individual as to the enormous prevalence[6] of this practice at this time.

The attempted abortion preclear may not be discovered to be such until considerable auditing has already been done. Any auditing done on an attempted abortion preclear, unless it is solely addressed to making the case workable, is wasted until the attempted abortions are reached.

The postbirth aberree presents a somewhat different case than the prenatal since his case can be entered at any point and the earliest moments of it can be attained easily. This is not true of the attempted abortion preclear. Attempted abortions may run to any number. Since they are easily the most prevalent dramatization of engrams in the society, they are repeated time

---

6. **prevalence:** widespread; of wide extent or occurrence; in general use or acceptance.

and again. The auditor will find it necessary to "unstack" the prenatal period. He will ordinarily reach the latest prenatal injury first. As he finds and examines it, it places itself on the time track. By going to earlier and earlier attempts, more and more of these engrams are revealed until at last the earliest is discovered. The auditor must be prepared to spend many hours of hard work in unstacking injuries. He will many times believe that he has reached the basic of that engram chain only to discover that another type of abortion was attempted prior to that moment. He need not address these engrams for any length of time before he goes on to the earlier one. He should only get some idea of them so that they will be easily locatable on the return. The basic engram on the attempted abortion case may be found shortly after the first missed period of the mother.

Its emotion will be exactly that of the person or persons attempting to perform the abortion. The prenatal human being identifies himself with himself but an adult returned to the prenatal period is reinterpreting the data and will find that he has and is confusing himself with other people associated in the attempts. This engramic data may have slumbered for years before it became violently restimulated and may indeed never have been awakened. It must be removed, however, before a Clear can be obtained. The auditor should be prepared to un-stack fifty or more incidents before birth if necessary.

When he is at last in the vicinity of the basic, even the most skeptical preclear (one who has skepticism as part of the prenatal engram chains) will have no further question as to what is happening to him. The auditor should be prepared to encounter difficulty in the ability of the preclear to hear voices or feel pain, as it is quite common for the engramic content to contain such phrases as "unconscious" and "can't see, can't feel, can't hear," this having been the misconception of the society regarding prenatal life.

The auditor should never be appalled at the damage the prenatal human being has received and so question the validity of his preclear's data. Unless the umbilical cord[7] is severed or the heart is stopped it is apparently the case that no damage, particularly in the earlier months, is too great for the organism to reconstruct.

In that parents performing abortions are usually dramatizing attempted abortions which have been performed on them, rationality of content in the engrams should not be expected. Even the data given for it by the abortionist father, mother or professional is often entirely inaccurate.

The test of an engram is whether or not it will lift and whether or not the somatics which accompanied it disappear and a tone 4 is obtained. Rearranging data into other sequences will not obtain this. The exact content must be brought out.

The attempted abortion human being is often struck unconscious by the earliest part of each attempt since the head is so available to the knitting needles, hat pins, orangewood sticks,[8] buttonhooks[9] and so forth which are employed. These periods of unconsciousness must be penetrated and will quite ordinarily release slowly.

The number of prenatal engrams should not particularly appall the auditor for when the basic has been discovered and a tone 4 achieved, the succeeding experiences will lift with greater

---

7. **umbilical cord:** cord connected to the navel of the fetus to supply nourishment prior to birth.

8. **orangewood sticks:** pointed sticks, originally made of orangewood, used in manicuring.

9. **buttonhooks:** small hooks for pulling buttons through buttonholes, as in some former shoes.

and greater ease. The periods of consciousness interspersed between the prenatal engrams, being locks, will vanish.

Birth is in itself a severe experience and is recorded by the human being from the first moments of pain throughout the entire experience. Everything in a birth is engramic since the human being conceives the ministrations[10] to be more or less antagonistic when they are accompanied by so much pain. A birth must be lifted as a matter of course but not until the presence or absence of prenatals have been established. Even after birth has been lifted, prenatals should be looked for, since prenatals may often be found only after birth has been exhausted. The habits of obstetricians,[11] the presence of sound and speech in the delivery room, the swabbing of an infant's nostrils, the examination of its mouth, the severe treatment administered to start its breathing and the drops in the eyes may account in themselves for many psychosomatic ills. A cough, however, although it is present in birth and seems to be alleviated by the exhaustion of the birth engram, is quite ordinarily blood running down the throat of the prenatal during an attempted abortion. Any perception during birth, when difficulty is encountered with breathing, may become a restimulator for asthma.[12] Clean fresh air and electric lights may cause allergies and may be the principal restimulators. Everything said during birth, as well as everything said during prenatal experiences, is recorded in the reactive mind and acts as aberrational matter which can and does cause psychological and physiological changes in the individual. Because the parents are not greatly in evidence at birth,

---

10. **ministrations:** acts or instances of giving help or care.

11. **obstetricians:** medical doctors who specialize in the branch of medicine concerned with the care and treatment of women during pregnancy, childbirth and the period immediately following.

12. **asthma:** a chronic disorder characterized by wheezing, coughing, difficulty in breathing and a suffocating feeling, usually caused by an allergy.

---

this experience may not be restimulated for many years. Prenatals, on the other hand, restimulate more easily.

Infant life is very sentient.[13] Delay in learning to talk is delay in learning the complexity of handling vocal muscles rather than a delay in ability to record. Everything in infant life is recorded and the engrams received in it are extremely valid.

The auditor will find himself dealing mainly with prenatal, birth, and infant life. The cases are very rare which have many important basics in childhood or adult life. These last periods contain mainly secondary engrams which, though they must be addressed to create the Clear, should not engage much initial attention on the part of the Dianeticist. Most of the experiences of mental anguish in childhood and adult life are founded on very early engrams and are locks which are almost self-removing.

Moments of unconsciousness which contain physical pain and conceived antagonism lying in childhood and adult life are serious and can produce aberration. Engram chains complete with basic may be found which will, all by themselves, exhaust.

---

13. **sentient:** of, having or capable of feeling or perception; conscious.

16

The "Laws" of Returning

16

The "Laws"
of Returning

By aberration is meant the aberree's reactions to and difficulties with his current environment.

By somatic is meant any physical or physically sensory abnormality which the preclear manifests generally or sporadically in his environment, or any such manifestation encountered and reexperienced in the process of auditing.

The aberration is the mental error caused by engrams and the somatic is the physical error occasioned by the same source.

The auditor follows the general rule that no aberrations or somatics exist in a subject which cannot be accounted for by engrams. He may ordinarily be expected to discover that anything which reduces the physical or mental perfection of the subject is engramic. He applies this rule first and in practice admits no organic trouble of any character. Only when he has obviously obtained a Clear and when he has observed and has had that Clear medically examined after a period of sixty days to six months from the end of auditing should he be content to assign anything to organic origin. He cannot be expected to know until the final examination exactly what somatic was not engramic. In other words, he must persistently adhere to one line of thought (that the preclear can be brought to mental and physical perfection) before he resigns any mental or physical error in the preclear to a purely organic category. Too little is known at this writing of the recoverability of the mind and body for a Dianeticist to deny that ability to recover. Since primary research, considerable practice has demonstrated that this ability to reconstruct and recover is enormous, far beyond anything previously conceived possible.

Dianetics accounts for *all* faith healing phenomena on an entirely scientific basis and the Dianeticist can expect himself to consort[1] daily in his practice with what appear to be miracles.

In addition to knowledge of his subject, considerable intelligence and imagination, and a personality which inspires confidence, the Dianetic auditor must possess persistency to a remarkable degree. In other words, his drives must be phenomenally high. There is no substitute for the auditor's having been cleared. It is possible for an individual to operate with Dianetics without having been released and he may do so for some time without repercussion, but as he audits he will most certainly encounter the perceptics contained in some of his own engrams time after time until these engrams are so restimulated that he will become mentally or physically ill.

In psychoanalysis[2] it was possible for the analyst to escape

---

1. **consort:** to keep company; associate.

2. **psychoanalysis:** a system of mental therapy developed by Sigmund Freud [(1856–1939) Austrian physician and neurologist: founder of psychoanalysis] in Austria in 1894 and which depends upon the following practices for its effects: The patient is made to talk about and recall his childhood for years while the practitioner brings about a transfer of the patient's personality to his own and searches for hidden sexual incidents, believed by Freud to be the only cause of aberration. The practitioner reads sexual significances into all statements and evaluates them for the patient along sexual lines. Each of these points later proved to be based on false premises and incomplete research, accounting for their lack of results and the subsequent failure of the subject and its offshoots.

this fate because he dealt primarily with locks occurring in the postspeech life. The analyst might even experience relief from operating on patients since it might clarify his own locks which were and more or less always had been completely available to his analytical mind. This is very far from the case with the Dianeticist who handles continually the vital and highly charged data which *cause* physical and mental aberrations. An auditor in Dianetics may work with impunity[3] for a very short time only before his own condition demands that he himself be audited. While this is aside from the main subject of auditing, it has been too often observed to be neglected.

Every engram possesses some quality which denies it to the analytical mind. There are roughly four types of denial. First there is the "self-locking" engram[4] which contains the species of phrases, "Frank will never know about this," "Forget it!" "Cannot remember it!" and so forth. Second is the "self-invalidating" engram which contains the species of the phrases, "Never happened," "Can't believe it," "Wouldn't possibly imagine it" and so on. Third is the preclear ejection engram[5] which contains the species of phrases, "Can't stay here," "Get out!" and other phrases which will not permit the preclear to remain in its vicinity but return him to present time. A fourth is the seizing engram[6] which contains the species of phrases, "Stay here," "Hold still," "Can't get out" and so on.

---

3. **impunity:** exemption from punishment, penalty or harm.

4. **''self-locking'' engram:** an engram containing commands which, literally translated, mean that the engram does not exist, such as "This is going nowhere," "I must not talk about it," etc.

5. **preclear ejection engram:** an engram containing such things as, "Don't ever come back," "I've got to stay away," etc., including any combination of words which *literally* mean ejection.

6. **seizing engram:** an engram containing a command which holds the preclear at a point on the time track, such as, "Don't leave me," "Hold on to this," "Don't let go," etc.

These four are the general types which the Dianeticist will find to occasion him the greatest difficulty. The type of phrase being encountered, however, is easily diagnosed from preclear reaction.

There are many other types of engrams and species of phrases which will be encountered. There is the "self-perpetuating" engram which implies that, "It will always be this way" and "It happens all the time." The auditor will soon learn to recognize them, forming lists of his own.

An engram would not be an engram unless it had strong compulsive or repressive data contained in it. All engrams are self-locking to some degree, being well off the time track and touching it slightly, if at all, with some minor and apparently innocuous[7] bit of information which the analytical mind disregards as unimportant. Classed with the self-locking specific variety are those phrases which deny perception of any kind. The Dianetic auditor will continually encounter perception denial and will find it one of the primary reasons the preclear cannot recall and articulate[8] the engram. "Can't see," "Can't hear," "Can't feel" and "Isn't alive" tend to self-lock the whole engram containing any such phrases.

As the engram is a powerful surcharge of physical pain, it will without any phrases whatsoever deny itself to the analytical mind which, in seeking to scan it, is repelled by its operating principle that it must avoid pain for the organism. As has already been covered, there are five ways the organism can handle a source of pain. It can neglect it, attack it, succumb to it, flee from it or avoid it. As the entire organism handles exterior pain sources, so does the analytical mind tend to react to engrams.

---

7. **innocuous:** that does not injure or harm; harmless.

8. **articulate:** to express clearly.

There is an exterior world reaction of the organism to pain sources then. This is approximated when the analytical mind is addressed in regard to engrams. There is an excellent reason for this. Everything contained in the reactive mind is exterior source material. The analytical mind was out of circuit and was recording imperfectly if at all in the time period when the exterior source was entered into the reactive mind.

An analytical mind when asked to approach an engram reacts as it would have had it been present, which is to say, in circuit, at the moment when the engram was being received. Therefore, an artificial approach to the engram must be made which will permit the auditor to direct the subject's analytical mind into but one source of action: Attack.

The actual incident must be located and reexperienced. In that the analytical mind has five possible ways of reacting to the engram and in that the auditor desires that only one of these— attack—be used, the preclear must be persuaded from using the remaining four.

On this general principle can be created many types of approach to the problem of obtaining a Clear. The one which is offered in this manual is that one which has met with quicker and more predictable results than others researched. It has given, in use, one hundred percent results. In the beginning, at this time, an auditor should not attempt to stray far from this offered technique. He should attempt to vary it only when he himself has had extensive and sufficient practice which will enable him to be very conversant with the nature of engrams. Better techniques will undoubtedly be established which will provide swifter exhaustion of the reactive mind. The offered technique has produced results in all types of cases so far encountered.

There are three equations which demonstrate how and why

the auditor and preclear can reach engrams and exhaust them:

I. The auditor's dynamics are equal to or less than the engramic surcharge in the preclear.

II. The preclear's dynamics are less than the engramic surcharge.

III. The auditor's dynamics plus the preclear's dynamics are greater than the engramic surcharge.

When the preclear's dynamics are entirely or almost entirely reduced, as in the case of amnesia trance, drug trances and so forth, the auditor's dynamics are not always sufficient to force the preclear's analytical mind into an attack upon the engram.

The auditor's dynamics directed against an engram in a preclear who has not been subjected to a process which will inhibit the free play of his reactive mind and concentrate it, ordinarily provokes the preclear into one of the four unusable methods of succumbing, fleeing, avoiding or neglecting the engram. Demanding that the preclear "face reality" or "see reason" or that he "stop his foolish actions" fall precisely into this category. The auditor's dynamics operating against an awake preclear can produce an "insanity break," temporary or of considerable duration in the preclear.

When the preclear is in reverie some of his own dynamics are present and the auditor's dynamics added to these make a combination sufficient to overcome the engramic surcharge.

If the auditor releases his dynamics *against* the analytical mind of the preclear, which is to say, the person of the preclear, while an attempt is being made to reach an engram (in violation of the Auditor's Code or with some erroneous idea that the whole person of the preclear is confronting him) he will receive in return all the fury of the engramic surcharge.

An engram can be dramatized innumerable times, for such is the character of the reactive mind that the surcharge of the engram cannot exhaust itself and will not exhaust itself regardless of its age or the number of times dramatized until it has been approached by the analytical mind of the subject.

The additive dynamic drive law must be made to apply before engrams are reached. It is very occasionally necessary to change Dianetic auditors, for some preclears will work well only with either a male or a female auditor or with one or another individual auditor. This will not be found necessary in many cases. Three cases are on record where the preclear was definitely antipathetic toward the auditor throughout the entire course of auditing. The Dianeticist was found to be a restimulator for one or more of the persons contained in the engrams. Even so, these persons responded. Greater patience was required on the part of the auditor. Closer observance of the Auditor's Code was necessary and a longer time was required for auditing. It will be discovered that once the preclear understands what is desired of him and why, his basic personality is aroused to the extent that it will cooperate with any auditor in order to be free. It will suffer through many violations of the Auditor's Code. Once a preclear has started his auditing he will ordinarily continue to cooperate in the major requirements to the fullest extent, no matter what apparent antagonisms he may display in minor matters.

Reverie is therefore the desirable method. The analytical mind of the preclear, while reduced in its potential and under direction, is still capable of thinking its own thoughts and form-ing its own opinions. Implicit[9] obedience to whatever the auditor suggests is not desirable as the preclear will inject extraneous material at the faintest suggestion of the auditor. Drugs inhibit the somatic and have no use in entering a case.

The fact that the Dianeticist is interested solely in what has been done *to* the preclear and is not at all interested in what the preclear himself has done to others greatly facilitates auditing since there is no social disgrace in having been an unwitting victim.

The preclear is placed in a light state of "concentration" which is not to be confused with hypnosis. In the state of alliance,[10] therefore, the mind of the preclear will be found to be, to some degree, detachable from his surroundings and directed interiorly. The first thing that the Dianeticist will discover in most preclears is aberration of the sense of time. There are various ways that he can circumvent this and construct a time track along which he can cause the preclear's mind to travel. Various early experiences which are easily reached are examined and an early diagnosis can be formed. Then begins an immedi-ate effort to reach basic, with attempted abortion or prenatal accident predominating.[11] Failures on the first attempts to reach prenatal experiences should not discourage the Dianetic auditor since many hours may be consumed and many false basics reached and exhausted before the true prenatal basic is attained.

In this type of reverie the Dianeticist can use and will observe certain apparently natural laws in force. They are as follows:

---

9. **implicit:** without reservation or doubt; unquestioning; absolute.

10. **alliance:** a merging of efforts or interests by persons, families, states or organi-zations.

11. **predominating:** being the stronger or leading element; prevailing.

The difficulties the analytical mind encounters when returned to or searching for an engram are identical to the command content of that engram.

An aberree in adult life is more or less obeying, as restimulated, the composite experiences contained in his engrams.

The preclear's behavior in reverie is regulated by the commands contained in the engram to which he is returned and is modified by the composite of chronologically preceding engrams on his time track.

The somatics of a preclear are at their highest in an engram where they were received and at the moment of reception in that experience.

When returned to a point prior to an engram, the commands and somatics of that engram are not effective on the preclear. As he is returned to the moment of an engram, the prelear experiences, as the common denominator of all engrams, a considerable lessening of his analytical potential. He speaks and acts in a modified version of the engram. All complaints he makes to the auditor should be regarded as possibly being verbatim from, first, the engram that he is reexperiencing, or second, from prior engrams.

At the precise moment of an engramic command the preclear experiences obedience to that command. The emotion a preclear experiences when regressed to an engram is identical to the emotional tone of that engram. Excesses of emotion will be found to be contained in the word content of the engram as commands.

When a preclear is returned to before the moment of reception of an engram he is not subject to any part of that engram, emotionally, aberrationally or somatically.

When the time track is found to contain loops or is blurred in any of its portions, its crossings or confusions are directly attributable to engramic commands which precisely state the confusion.

Any difficulty a preclear may experience with returning, reaching engrams, perceiving or recounting, are directly and precisely commanded by engrams.

An engram would not be an engram were it easy to reach, gave the preclear no difficulty and contained no physical pain.

The characteristic of engrams is confusion: first, the confusion of the time track; second, the confusion of an engram chain wherein similar words or somatics mix incidents; third, confusion of incidents with engrams.

This confusion is occasioned by the disconnected state of the analytical mind during the receipt of the engram. Auditing by location and identification of hidden incidents, first rebuilds at least the early part of the time track, locates and fixes engrams in relation to one another in time and then locates the basic of the basic chain and exhausts it. The remainder of the chain must also be exhausted. The secondaries exhaust with ease after the erasure of the basic or the basic of any chain (within that chain). Locks vanish without being located. A tone 4 gained on basic permits the subsequent erasure on the time track to go forward with ease. A whole chain may rise to 4 without the basic *chain* having been located.

Any perception of prespeech life during reverie denotes the existence of engramic experience as far back as the time track is open.

If the individual's general tone is not clearly tone 4, if he is still interested in his engrams, another more basic chain than the one found still exists.

Engramic patterns tend to form an avoidance pattern for the preclear. From basic outward there is an observable and progressive divergence[12] between the person himself and his returned self. In the basic engram of the basic chain and for a few subsequent incidents on that chain, he will be found within himself and receiving the experiences as himself. In subsequent incidents cleavage[13] is observable, and in late engrams the preclear is found to be observing the action from outside of himself, almost as a disinterested party. This forms the principal primary test for the basic of the basic chain. Another test for basic is "sag."

Any engram may be exhausted to a point where it will recede without reaching tone 4. Although it is temporarily and momentarily lost to the individual and apparently does not trouble him, that engram which has been exhausted in a chain without the basic having been reached will "sag" or reappear within twenty-four to sixty hours. Basic on any chain will not sag but will lift on a number of recountings, rise to tone 4 and will remain erased. Another test for basic is whether or not it begins to lift with ease. If an engram does not intensify or remain static[14] after many recountings, it can be conceived to be at least a basic on some chain. Locks will lift and disappear without returning as they are not fixed by physical pain. Large numbers of locks can be exhausted bringing an alleviation of the preclear's difficulties and such a course may occasionally be pursued in the

---

12. **divergence:** a becoming different in form or kind.

13. **cleavage:** the state of being split or divided.

14. **static:** not changing.

entrance of a case. The discovery and lifting of the basic to which the locks are appended removes the locks automatically.

These rules and laws, even if modified in their statement, will be found invariable. Incompetent auditing cannot be excused by the supposed discovery of a special case or exception. A physical derangement must be in the category of actually missing parts of the organism to cause permanent disability, and instances of this are not common.

17

Case Histories

17

Case Histories

The following case histories have been selected at random. Due to lack of time, these case histories are Releases, not Clears. The Releases have been fully diagnosed and researched.

Case No. 1
Hypertension,[1] Combat Fatigue[2]
Tuberculosis,[3] Arrested
Myopic[4] Astigmatism[5]

A forty-three-year-old ex-army officer and author; inclined to petty tyrannies;[6] twice divorced; no children. Processed by Army as psychoneurotic.

Birth was discovered immediately but would not satisfactorily release. The preclear experienced great difficulty in visualizing and his aberrations intensified during auditing.

1. **hypertension:** abnormally high blood pressure, or a disease of which this is the chief sign.

2. **combat fatigue:** a mental disorder due to stress in wartime combat.

3. **tuberculosis:** an infectious disease that may affect almost any tissue of the body, especially the lungs.

4. **myopic:** nearsighted (seeing distinctly at a short distance only).

5. **astigmatism:** a defect in an eye or lens preventing proper focusing.

6. **tyrannies:** oppressive, severe and unjust dominations.

By use of dreams and restimulation of somatics the preclear was able to reach the beginning of the engramic chain as counted backwards from birth. Fifteen prenatal experiences were unstacked. They were found lying in two loops. The loops were corrected and the basic engram of the basic chain was reached. (A loop is a redoubling of the time track back on itself. In this case incidents are not in their correct place on the time track.)

The basic consisted of a severe quarrel between his mother and father with several abdominal blows being received by the mother. The mother was protesting that it would make her sick all of her life. At the same time the mother was coughing from a throat blow. The father was insisting that he was master in his own home and that people had to do what he told them. This quarrel occurred at about 4½ months after conception and resulted in the temporary paralysis of the preclear's right side. The remainder of the chain consisted of similar incidents, evidently dramatizations on the part of the father of his own engrams, as the words used were almost identical, one engram to the next. This chain accounted for and relieved the subject's fear that he would be ill and his desire to tyrannize others.

Birth was then found to consist of near suffocation and considerable antagonism between the doctor and the nurse. This was registered as commands to himself to the effect that he was blind and could not see. Birth was in the home and dust, camphor, the smell of clean sheets and greased metal were the restimulators for this severe lung irritation. This birth was not restimulated until the age of five and the prenatals were not restimulated until entrance into the service when the need for authority manifested itself.

No locks were found to need attention and only one half-hour of his war experience failed to release, that being a new basic.

Number of hours on case: fifty-five.

Case No. 2
Apathy, preclear had been under psychiatric treatment for two years prior to Dianetic auditing. She had experienced no relief. Malnutrition.

An eighteen-year-old girl in a condition of apathy bordering upon a break and regularly worsening. She had been recently married. Afraid of her husband. She had done very badly in school, sporadically engaged in sexual escapades, relapsing afterwards into an illness which was variously diagnosed.

Case was entered with ease. Birth was reached and would not exhaust. A search for prenatals was for ten hours fruitless, until certain somatics were artificially restimulated and intensified to the point that the preclear had to recall the incident to find relief. Eight prenatals were then unstacked and only two incidents were discovered in confusion with each other, held together with a head somatic.

The basic proved to be a mutual abortion attempt by the mother and father. The mother said that she would die if anyone found out but that she would probably die anyway. The father said that the baby was probably like her and that he didn't want it. Eighteen penetrations of the head, throat and shoulders with a long orangewood stick—probably in the third month. Several similar incidents completed this chain. Coitus followed each attempt at abortion. Another incident proved to be a basic without a chain and with innumerable locks: an attempted abortion by a professional abortionist who used some form of needle and scraper. Birth was found to be a mild experience. Three infant engrams with their own basic were discovered. They consisted of the mother's fear over the injury and the fear that the baby would die.

Contagion of attempted abortion engrams was particularly manifest in the mother's neurotic dwelling on fear of death, which was obviously a dramatization.

All neurotic and psychotic symptoms were relieved with a marked improvement in the health of the preclear and an increase of twenty-seven points on the Army Alpha Test.[7]

Time of work: sixty-five hours.

Case No. 3
Psychotic murderous rages.
Chronic skin rash.

A thirty-year-old male negro, six feet four inches in height, about two hundred and fifty pounds—swamp worker. He was in continual trouble with police and had a considerable jail record. He continually dramatized a hatred of women. He also dramatized a continuous suspicion that he was about to be murdered. His IQ was about eighty-five.

Uniquely enough, this case offered no difficulties in entrance. The subject was extremely cooperative with the Dianeticist. Birth was found and exhausted without improvement in the case. A number of infant and childhood engrams were discovered and tested. Continual address of the preclear's attention to prenatal life finally brought about a convulsion[8] in which terror and rage alternated. The Dianeticist was able to induce the preclear to listen to the voices he was hearing and to go through with the experience.

7. **Army Alpha Test:** a written intelligence test, developed by the U.S. Army in 1917 for measuring the intelligence of new recruits.

8. **convulsion:** a violent, involuntary contraction or spasm of the muscles.

The convulsion proved to be twenty engrams nearer birth than the basic, which laid on another chain and which was discovered by dream technique. The convulsion was caused by the dramatization of an engram involving the injection of turpentine into the uterus by the mother in an attempted abortion. The main engramic chain consisted of the mother's efforts to abort herself. From engramic content it was gathered that the mother was a prostitute, for as many as twenty experiences of coitus succeeded two of these abortion attempts. They were too numerous to be evaluated.

The basic chain contained many quarrels about money between the mother and her customers. The somatics of this chain were largely bruises and concussions caused by the mother ramming herself into pointed objects or beating her stomach and abdomen. There were many loops in the basic chain caused by the similarity of incident and the confusion of coitus with abortion attempts. The basic incident was at last discovered and exhausted. It was found to lie about twenty days after conception, when the mother first discovered her pregnancy.

All engrams were exhausted in the basic chain. The convulsion was fully cleared and birth was suddenly found to have been a very painful experience, particularly because the child was taken by others immediately after birth. Only one engram chain (unconsciousness resulting from fist fights) was found in childhood.

About the Author

About the Author

L. Ron Hubbard is acclaimed by millions as the foremost author of self-betterment books in the world today, primarily because his works express a firsthand knowledge of the nature of man—knowledge gained not from standing on the sidelines but through lifelong experience with people from all walks of life.

As Ron said, "One doesn't learn about life by sitting in an ivory tower, thinking about it. One learns about life by being part of it." And that is how he lived.

He began his quest for knowledge on the nature of man at a very early age. When he was eight years old he was already well on his way to being a seasoned traveler, covering a quarter of a million miles by the age of nineteen. His adventures included voyages to China, Japan and other points in the Orient and South Pacific. During this time he became closely acquainted with twenty-one different races in areas all over the world.

After returning to the United States, Ron pursued his formal studies of mathematics and engineering at George Washington University, where he was also a member of one of the first classes ever taught on nuclear physics. He realized that neither the Eastern understanding of spiritual matters nor Western scientific knowledge of the material universe contained the full answer to the problems of existence. Despite all of mankind's advances in the physical sciences, a *workable* technology of the mind and life had never been developed. The mental "technologies" which did exist, psychology and psychiatry, were actually barbaric, false subjects—no more workable than the methods of jungle witch doctors. Ron shouldered the responsibility of filling this gap in the knowledge of mankind.

He financed his early research through fiction writing. He became one of the most highly demanded and read authors in the golden age of popular adventure and science fiction writing during the 1930s and 1940s, interrupted only by his service in the U.S. Navy during World War II.

The war's end found Ron at Oak Knoll Naval Hospital, physically disabled. Applying what he had learned from his researches thus far, he began working with the casualties in the hospital. He made breakthroughs and developed techniques enabling him to help others to regain their health, to the mystery of the doctors, and bring about his own physical recovery. It was from this intensive research that the basic tenets of Dianetics technology were codified.

A year later, in 1948, he wrote the first formal manuscript detailing his discoveries. He did not offer it for publication at that time, but gave copies to friends who further copied it and passed it on to their friends. As a result, this first manuscript on Ron's breakthroughs and developments of Dianetics was passed around the world, all on its own power. The news of Dianetics spread like wildfire. Later published under the title *The Dynamics of Life*, Ron's first work on the subject of Dianetics caused a worldwide reaction which has not ceased to this day.

The interest generated by this manuscript prompted a flood

of requests for more information on the subject. Soon the demand for more details was so great that Ron found himself spending all his time answering letters about his discoveries and advances. He therefore decided to write a comprehensive text on the subject, *Dianetics: The Modern Science of Mental Health.*

With the publication of *Dianetics* on 9 May 1950, a complete handbook for the application of Ron's new technology was broadly available for the first time. More than 750 Dianetics study groups sprang up within a few short months of its publication.

Following the release of this phenomenal bestseller, Ron was in even greater demand for lectures, demonstrations and more information on Dianetics. He was called upon to expand the subject and to answer an ever-increasing avalanche of questions. Ron launched into further research and kept the public informed of his new discoveries through lectures and a flood of published bulletins, magazines and books.

Ron's work did not stop with the successes of Dianetics. Further research led him to the basic truths of life itself and from these discoveries he developed Scientology, the first totally workable technology for the improvement of life.

The number of books and lectures continued to grow for more than three decades as Ron kept on with his research into the mind and life.

Today Ron's works—including an astounding number of books, taped lectures, instructional films, writings, demonstrations and briefings—are studied and applied daily. Dianetics and Scientology techniques are used in hundreds of Hubbard Dianetics Foundations and Scientology organizations on every continent.

It all began with this first manuscript, *The Dynamics of Life.*

With his research fully completed and codified, L. Ron Hubbard departed his body on 24 January 1986.

Ron's work opened a new door for mankind. Through his efforts, there now exists a totally workable technology with which people can help each other improve their lives and succeed in achieving their goals.

Millions of people all over the world consider they have no truer friend.

Glossary

Abbreviate: to shorten by cutting off a part; to cut short.

aberrations: departures from rational thought or behavior. From the Latin, *aberrare*, to wander from; Latin, *ab*, away, *errare*, to wander. It means basically to err, to make mistakes, or more specifically to have fixed ideas which are not true. The word is also used in its scientific sense. It means departure from a straight line. If a line should go from A to B, and it is "aberrated" it would go from A to some other point, to some other point, to some other point, to some other point, to some other point and finally arrive at B. Taken in its scientific sense, it would also mean the lack of straightness or to see crookedly as, for example, a man sees a horse but thinks he sees an elephant. Aberrated conduct would be wrong conduct, or conduct not supported by reason. Aberration is opposed to sanity which would be its opposite.

aberree: an aberrated person.

abyss: anything too deep for measurement; profound depth.

acute: severe, but of short duration.

aggregation: a group, body or mass composed of many distinct parts.

allayed: lessened, relieved or alleviated.

allergies: conditions of excessive sensitivity to specific substances such as foods, pollens, dust, etc., or conditions (as heat or cold) which in similar amounts are harmless to most people; they are manifested in physiological disorders.

alliance: a merging of efforts or interests by persons, families, states or organizations.

amentias: conditions of feeblemindedness or mental deficiency.

amnesia: partial or total loss of memory caused by brain injury or by shock, repression, etc.

analogy: explanation of something by comparing it point by point with something similar.

anatomy: the structure of an animal or plant or any of its parts.

antipathetic: opposed or antagonistic in character, tendency, etc.

apprised: informed or notified.

approximation: a state of coming or getting close to or resembling.

Army Alpha Test: a written intelligence test, developed by the U.S. Army in 1917 for measuring the intelligence of new recruits.

articulate: to express clearly.

asthma: a chronic disorder characterized by wheezing, coughing, difficulty in breathing and a suffocating feeling, usually caused by an allergy.

astigmatism: a defect in an eye or lens preventing proper focusing.

attendantly: in a manner accompanying as a circumstance or result.

attuned: adjusted; brought into harmony or agreement.

audio: of hearing or sound.

auditing: the application of Dianetics processes and procedures to someone by a trained auditor.

auditor: a person trained and qualified in applying Dianetics processes and procedures to individuals for their betterment; called an auditor because *auditor* means "one who listens."

auto-control: autohypnosis or an attempt to process oneself without an auditor. If attempted in Dianetics, autohypnosis is probably as close to fruitless masochism as one can get. If a patient places himself in autohypnosis and regresses himself in an effort to reach illness or birth or prenatals, the only thing he will get is ill.

axioms: statements of natural laws on the order of those of the physical sciences.

basic: the earliest engram on an engram chain.

buttonhooks: small hooks for pulling buttons through buttonholes, as in some former shoes.

capriciously: in a manner characterized by or subject to whim; impulsively or unpredictably.

cathode ray tube: a vacuum tube, for example, a television picture tube, in which beams of electrons are directed against a fluorescent screen where they produce a luminous image.

chain: a series of incidents of similar types.

charge: the quantity of electricity or electrical energy in or upon an object or substance.

charlatan: a person who pretends to knowledge or skill; quack.

Child Dianetics: that branch of Dianetics which is concerned with promoting optimum survival of the immature human organism until such time as standard procedure for adults may be employed.

chronically: in a continuing manner; constantly.

clairvoyance: the ability to perceive things that are not in sight or that cannot be seen.

cleavage: the state of being split or divided.

combat fatigue: a mental disorder due to stress in wartime combat.

common denominator: a characteristic, element, etc., held in common.

company: any relatively small group of soldiers.

complexion: general appearance or nature; character; aspect.

compulsions: irresistible, repeated, irrational impulses to perform some act.

connective tissue: tissue found throughout the body, serving to bind together and support other tissues and organs.

consolidating: making or becoming strong, stable, firmly established, etc.

consort: to keep company; associate.

contagion: communication or transfer from one to another.

contemporary: up-to-date.

convulsion: a violent, involuntary contraction or spasm of the muscles.

cosmic: of the universe.

cursorily: in a hastily done manner; done rapidly with little attention to detail.

deism: belief in the existence of a God on purely rational grounds without reliance on revelation or authority; especially, the 17th and 18th century doctrine that God created the world and its natural laws, but takes no further part in its functioning.

delineated: explained in words; described.

delusions: beliefs in things that are contrary to fact or reality, resulting from deception, misconception or mental disorder.

demarked: limited or distinguished.

denote: be a sign of; indicate.

deranged: upset in arrangement, order or operation; unsettled; disordered.

despondency: loss of courage or hope; dejection.

detriment: loss, damage, disadvantage or injury.

developed: made known or apparent; disclosed.

diagnostic: of or constituting a careful examination and analysis of the facts in an attempt to understand or explain something.

Dianetics® spiritual healing technology: man's most advanced school of the mind. *Dianetics* means "through the soul" (from Greek *dia*, through, and *noos*, soul). *Dianetics* is further defined as "what the soul is doing to the body." It is a way of handling the energy of which life is made in such a way as to bring about a greater efficiency in the organism and in the spiritual life of the individual.

Dickens, Charles: (1812–70) English novelist of the late 19th century whose books are noted for picturesque and extravagant characters in the lower economic strata of England at that time.

dictates: guiding principles or requirements.

differential: a difference between comparable things.

dire: dreadful; terrible.

discounted: disregarded partly or wholly.

dispersion: state or condition of being scattered, driven or sent in different directions.

divergence: a becoming different in form or kind.

dramatis personae: the characters in a play or story (used here to refer to people present in the engrams of the aberree).

dramatizations: repetitions in action of what has happened to one in experience; replays now of something that happened in the past, out of their time and period.

dynamic principle of existence: is *Survive!* No behavior or activity has been found to exist without this principle. It is not new that life is surviving. It is new that life has as its entire dynamic urge only survival.

eccentricities: deviations from what is ordinary or customary, as in conduct or manner; oddities; unconventionalities.

Educational Dianetics: contains the body of organized knowledge necessary to train minds to their optimum efficiency and to an optimum of skill and knowledge in the various branches of the works of man.

eidetic: designating or of mental images that are unusually vivid and almost photographically exact.

electrons: particles of matter with a negative electric charge.

elicit: to draw out (information, a response, etc.).

embraced: included; contained.

emote: to give expression to emotion.

emphatically: decidedly; decisively.

encephalograph: an instrument for measuring and recording the electric activity of the brain.

engrams: moments of pain and "unconsciousness" containing physical pain or painful emotion and all perceptions, and not available to the analytical mind as experience.

enjoined: urged or imposed with authority; ordered; enforced.

equivocal: suspicious; questionable.

erasure: the action of going over and describing the content of an engram until it has vanished entirely.

eugenic: pertaining or adapted to the production of fine offspring especially in the human race.

exhaustion: the act of drawing out or draining off completely.

facet: any of a number of sides or aspects, as of a personality.

fetus: in man, the offspring in the womb from the end of the third month of pregnancy until birth.

finite: having measurable or definable limits.

flagrant: very bad and obvious.

flank: the right or left side of a body of troops, etc.

forebears: ancestors.

forgetter: any engram command which makes the individual believe he can't remember.

frontal lobe: portion of the brain behind the forehead.

genetic: pertaining to the line of father and mother to child, grown child to new child and so forth.

geometrical progression: progression with a constant ratio between successive quantities, as 1:3:9:27:81.

germane: truly relevant; pertinent; to the point.

glandular: derived from or affected by organs in the body that secrete substances to be used in other parts of the body or expelled from it.

gleans: collects or gathers anything little by little or slowly.

guile: slyness and cunning in dealing with others; craftiness.

hectic: characterized by confusion, rush, excitement, etc.

heuristically: in a manner serving to find out; specifically applied to a system of education under which the student is trained to find out things for himself.

hitherto: until this time.

hormones: substances formed in some organ of the body (glands) and carried by a body fluid to another organ or tissue, where it has a specific effect.

hypertension: abnormally high blood pressure, or a disease of which this is the chief sign.

hypnotic: tending to produce sleep or a trance.

hysterias: outbreaks of wild, uncontrolled excitement or feeling, such as fits of laughing and crying.

illusions: false perceptions, conceptions or interpretations of what one sees.

implanted: planted firmly or deeply, embedded.

implicit: without reservation or doubt; unquestioning; absolute.

impunity: exemption from punishment, penalty or harm.

inanimate: (of rocks and other objects) lifeless, (of plants) lacking animal life.

indiscriminate: not recognizing the differences between; not making careful choices or distinctions.

infatuation: the condition of being inspired with foolish or shallow love or affection.

inherent: existing in something as a natural or permanent characteristic or quality.

innate: existing naturally rather than acquired; that seems to have been in one from birth.

innocuous: that does not injure or harm; harmless.

instinct: an inborn impulse or tendency to perform certain acts or behave in certain ways.

insulin shocks: states of collapse caused by a decrease in blood sugar resulting from the administration of excessive insulin.

integration: the organization of various traits, feelings, attitudes, etc., into one harmonious personality.

interspersed: scattered among other things; put here and there or at intervals.

intimidated: made timid or afraid.

introverts: directs (one's interest, mind or attention) upon one-self.

Judicial Dianetics: covers the field of judgment within the society and amongst the societies of man. Of necessity it embraces jurisprudence (science or philosophy of law) and its codes and establishes precision definitions and equations for the establishment of equity. It is the science of judgment.

keynote: the basic idea or ruling principle.

keys: things that secure or control entrance to a place, or provide access to something.

kingdoms: the three great divisions into which all natural objects have been classified (the animal, vegetable and mineral kingdoms).

libidos: sexual urges or instincts.

lifted: raised and vanished; dispelled.

locks: analytical moments in which the perceptics of the engram are approximated, thus restimulating the engram or bringing it into action, the present-time perceptics being erroneously interpreted by the reactive mind to mean that the same condition which produced physical pain once before is now again at hand.

maladjustments: examples of lack of harmony between the individual and his environment.

malady: a disease, illness or sickness (used figuratively).

manic: a person whose life force is channeled straight through an engram and whose behavior, no matter how enthusiastic or euphoric, is actually highly aberrated.

manifestation: something which is are apparent to the senses; something which shows itself.

ministrations: acts or instances of giving help or care.

mutation: change or alteration in form.

myopic: nearsighted (seeing distinctly at a short distance only).

narcosynthesis: drug hypnotism.

natural selection: a process in nature resulting in the survival and perpetuation of only those forms of plant and animal life having certain favorable characteristics that best enable them to adapt to a specific environment.

nebulous: unclear; vague; indefinite.

neurasthenia: a type of neurosis characterized by irritability, fatigue, weakness, anxiety and, often, localized pains or distress without apparent physical causes: formerly thought to result from weakness or exhaustion of the nervous system.

neuroses: emotional states containing conflicts and emotional data inhibiting the abilities or welfare of the individual.

nitrous oxide: a colorless, nonflammable gas used as an anesthetic and in aerosols.

noble: very good or excellent; superior of its kind.

obstetricians: medical doctors who specialize in the branch of medicine concerned with the care and treatment of women during pregnancy, childbirth and the period immediately following.

obtains: is in force or in effect; prevails.

occasioned: caused; brought about.

olfactory: the sense of smell.

orangewood sticks: pointed sticks, originally made of orangewood, used in manicuring.

pathologically: in a manner due to or involving disease.

patter: the talk of a group or class.

perceptics: sense messages.

philosophy: the love or pursuit of wisdom, or of knowledge of things and their causes, whether theoretical or practical.

phraseology: choice and pattern of words; way of speaking or writing.

physio: a portion of a word meaning "physical."

physiology: the organic processes or functions of an organism or any of its parts.

pitch: that quality of a tone or sound determined by the frequency of vibration of the sound waves reaching the ear: the greater the frequency, the higher the pitch.

Political Dianetics: embraces the field of group activity and organization to establish the optimum conditions and processes of leadership and intergroup relations.

poses: puts forward; presents.

positive suggestion: suggestion by the operator to a hypnotized subject with the sole end of creating a changed mental condition in the subject by implantation of the suggestion alone. It is the transplantation of something in the hypnotist's mind into the patient's mind. The patient is then to believe it and take it as part of himself.

posthypnotic: of, having to do with or carried out in the period following a hypnotic trance.

precariously: in a manner dependent on chance circumstances, unknown conditions or uncertain developments; uncertainly.

preclear: any person who has been entered into Dianetics processing. A person who, through Dianetics processing, is finding out more about himself and life.

preclear ejection engram: an engram containing such things as "Don't ever come back," "I've got to stay away," etc., including any combination of words which *literally* mean ejection.

precursors: earlier engrams.

predominating: being the stronger or leading element; prevailing.

prefrontal lobotomies: operations on the prefrontal lobes of the brain.

prejudicial: tending to injure or impair.

prenatal: existing or taking place before birth.

prevalence: widespread; of wide extent or occurrence; in general use or acceptance.

processes: sets of questions asked by an auditor to help a person find out more about himself or life.

processing: *see* **auditing.**

procreating: bringing (a living thing) into existence by the natural process of reproduction.

progeny: children, descendants or offspring collectively.

promiscuity: having casual, random sexual relations.

proviso: a condition or qualification.

psychic: of or having to do with the psyche (the spirit) or mind.

psychoanalysis: a system of mental therapy developed by Sigmund Freud [(1856–1939) Austrian physician and neurologist: founder of psychoanalysis] in Austria in 1894 and which depends upon the following practices for its effects: The patient is made to talk about and recall his childhood for years while the practitioner brings about a transfer of the patient's personality to his own and searches for hidden sexual incidents, believed by Freud to be the only cause of aberration. The practitioner reads sexual significances into all statements and evaluates them for the patient along sexual lines. Each of these points later proved to be based on false premises and incomplete research, accounting for their lack of results and the subsequent failure of the subject and its offshoots.

psychology: the study of the human brain and stimulus-response mechanisms. Its code word was "Man, to be happy, must adjust to his environment." In other words, man, to be happy, must be a total effect.

psychoneurotic: neurotic: a person who is mainly harmful to himself by reason of his aberrations, but not to the point of suicide.

psychoses: conflicts of commands which seriously reduce the individual's ability to solve his problems in his environment to a point where he cannot adjust some vital phase of his environmental needs.

psychosomatic: *psycho* refers to mind and *somatic* refers to body; the term *psychosomatic* means the mind making the body ill or illnesses which have been created physically within the body by derangement of the mind.

pusillanimity: lacking of courage; cowardliness.

rationalized: explained or interpreted on rational grounds.

raving: talking wildly or furiously, talking nonsensically in delirium; *raving mad*, completely mad.

reactive: irrational, reacting instead of acting.

reactive mind: the portion of the mind which works on a stimulus-response basis (given a certain stimulus it will automatically give a certain response) which is not under a person's volitional control and which exerts force and power over a person's awareness, purposes, thoughts, body and actions.

reactive thought: identity thought. The reactive mind is distinguished by the fact that although it thinks, it thinks wholly in identities. For instance, to the reactive mind under certain conditions there would be no difference between a microphone and a table.

rebuffed: bluntly or abruptly rejected, as of a person's advances.

regressed: gone back; returned; moved backward.

regression: a technique by which part of the individual's self remained in the present and part went back to the past.

reiterated: repeated (something done or said); said or done again or repeatedly.

repressions: commands that the organism must not do something.

resilient: recovering readily from illness, depression, adversity or the like.

resolve: to change or transform.

resolve: to determine or decide upon (a course of action, etc.).

retire: to return; to come back.

returned: the person has "sent" a portion of his mind to a past period on either a mental or combined mental and physical basis and can reexperience incidents which have taken place in his past in the same fashion and with the same sensations as before.

reverie: a light state of "concentration" not to be confused with hypnosis; in reverie the person is fully aware of what is taking place.

reverses: changes from good fortune to bad; defeats.

revivify: to relive an incident or some portion of it as if it were happening now.

sag: loss of firmness, strength or intensity; weakening through weariness, age, etc.

school: a group of people held together by the same teachings, beliefs, opinions, methods, etc.

Scientology: Scientology applied religious philosophy. It is the study and handling of the spirit in relationship to itself, universes and life. *Scientology* means *scio,* knowing in the fullest sense of the word and *logos,* to study. In itself the word means literally *knowing how to know.* Scientology is a "route," a way, rather than a dissertation or an assertive body of knowledge. Through its drills one may find the truth for himself. The technology is therefore not expounded as something to believe, but something to *do.*

scrutiny: a close examination; minute inspection.

secondary engrams: engrams which are engrams of the same character and kind and on the same drive line as the basic engram of a chain. An engram chain is then composed of a basic engram and a series of secondary engrams.

seizing engram: an engram containing a command which holds the preclear at a point on the time track, such as "Don't leave me," "Hold on to this," "Don't let go," etc.

self-determinism: a condition of determining the actions of self; the ability to direct oneself.

''self-locking'' engram: an engram containing commands which, literally translated, mean that the engram does not exist, such as "This is going nowhere," "I must not talk about it," etc.

semantic: of or pertaining to meaning, especially meaning in language.

semantics: the scientific study of the meanings and the development of meanings of words.

sensory strip: the sequential physical record of pain or discomfort of any kind from conception to present time.

sentient: of, having or capable of feeling or perception; conscious.

somatic: body sensation, illness or pain or discomfort. *Soma* means body.

somnambulistic: trancelike.

sporadic: happening from time to time; not constant or regular; occasional.

static: not changing.

subbrains: such parts of the body as the "funny bones" or any "judo sensitive" spots: the sides of the neck, the inside of the wrist, the places the doctors tap to find out if there is a reflex. These are subbrains picked up on the evolutionary line.

succumb: to give way (to); yield; submit.

superimposed: laid or placed (a thing) on top of something else.

supplants: takes the place of; supersedes, especially through force or plotting.

surcharge: an additional or excessive load or burden.

sustenance: food itself, nourishment.

syllabic: having to do with words or portions of words uttered as a single uninterrupted sound.

symbiotes: any or all life or energy forms which are mutually dependent for survival.

sympathetic: showing favor, approval or agreement.

tactile: of, having or related to the sense of touch.

tantrums: violent, willful outbursts of annoyance, rage, etc.; childish fits of bad temper.

telepathy: communication between minds by some means other than sensory perception.

tenacity: the quality or state of being persistent or stubborn.

tenet: a principle or belief held as a truth, as by some group.

theta: the symbol (Greek letter θ, *theta*) which represents thought, life force, the spirit or soul.

timbre: the characteristic or quality of sound that distinguishes one voice or musical instrument from another.

time track: consists of all the consecutive moments of "now" from the earliest moment of life of the organism to present time.

Tone Scale: the scale of emotional states which range from death at the bottom, up through apathy, grief, fear, covert hostility, anger, antagonism, boredom, conservatism, cheerfulness, to enthusiasm at the top.

trance: to put in a half-conscious state, seemingly between sleeping and waking, in which ability to function voluntarily may be suspended.

trite: worn out by constant use; no longer having freshness, originality or novelty; stale.

tuberculosis: an infectious disease that may affect almost any tissue of the body, especially the lungs.

tyrannies: oppressive, severe and unjust dominations.

umbilical cord: cord connected to the navel of the fetus to supply nourishment prior to birth.

unimpeded: not possessed of engrams.

vices: evil or wicked actions, habits or characteristics.

virtues: ideal qualities in good human conduct.

visio: the perception of light waves.

vocational: designating or of education, training, etc., intended to prepare one for an occupation, sometimes specifically in a trade.

weight: influence, power or authority.

Index

A = A = A, 71

aberrated information, 130; *see also* **reactive mind**

aberration(s), aberrated,
    attempted abortion and, 131
    cause and nature of, 18, 21–22, 48, 57
    contagion of, 117–118, 156
    defined, 45, 139
    dynamics and, 28, 35
    environment, aberration of, 119
    engrams and, 59, 71
    forms of, 59
    holding onto, 34, 78
    physical, 60
    relation to somatics, 45
    severity of, 45

aberree; *see* **preclear**

abortion, attempted; *see* **attempted abortion**

accidents, minor, 76

additive dynamic drive law, 145

affinity,
    becoming infatuation, 91
    establishment of, 86
    is a survival factor, 25
    maintaining, 90

alleviation, 126

amentias, 116

analyst, 140

analytical mind; *see also* **reactive mind; physio-animal mind**
    abnormal behavior of, 57
    assisting of preclear's, 95
    attempt of, to explain aberration, 43
    description of, 20–21
    disconnection of, 148
    dispersion of, 22, 53
    engram cannot be reached by, 41, 69, 72, 141
    five ways to handle danger or pain source, 71, 142
    hidden influence on, 41
    lock can be reached by, 46
    only way to aberrate, 74
    paralyzed by hypnotic drugs, 96
    protected by fuse system, 22
    reduction of awareness potential of, 41, 82, 83
    restoration of ability of, 58
    superimposed on brain, 10

analytical power, 51

analyzer, *see* **analytical mind**

anesthetics, 96

antipathies, 76

"appreciator," 72

artistry, 35

"assist engram," 83–84

asthma, 135

astigmatism, myopic, 153

Books and Tapes
by L. Ron Hubbard

To obtain any of the following materials by L. Ron Hubbard, contact the organization nearest you or order directly from the publisher. These addresses are given at the very back of this publication. Many of these works have been translated and are available in a number of different languages.

The works are arranged in the suggested order that they be read (or listened to), within each category.

Basic Dianetics Books

Dianetics: The Modern Science of Mental Health • Acclaimed as the most effective self-help book ever published. Dianetics technology has helped millions reach new heights of freedom and ability. Over 11,000,000 copies sold! Discover the source of mental barriers that prevent you from achieving your goals—and how to handle them!

Self Analysis • The complete do-it-yourself handbook for anyone who wants to improve their abilities and success potential. Use the simple, easy-to-learn techniques in *Self Analysis* to build self-confidence and reduce stress.

Dianetics: The Evolution of a Science • It is estimated that we use less than ten percent of our mind's potential. What stops us from developing and using the full potential of our minds? *Dianetics: The Evolution of a Science* is L. Ron Hubbard's incredible story of how he discovered the reactive mind and how he developed the keys to unlock its secrets. Get this firsthand account of what the mind really is, and how you can release its hidden potential.

Dianetics Graduate Books

Science of Survival • If you ever wondered why people act the way they do, you'll find this book a wealth of information. It's vital to anyone who wants to understand others and improve personal relationships. *Science of Survival* is built around a remarkable chart—The Hubbard Chart of Human Evaluation. With it you can understand and predict other people's behavior and reactions and greatly increase your control over your own life. This is a valuable handbook that can make a difference between success and failure on the job and in life.

Dianetics 55! • Your success in life depends on your ability to communicate. Do you know a formula exists for communication? Learn the rules of better communication that can help you live a more fulfilling life. Here, L. Ron Hubbard deals with the fundamental principles of communication and how you can master these to achieve your goals.

Child Dianetics • Here is a revolutionary new approach to rearing children with the techniques of Dianetics technology. Find out how you can help your child achieve greater confidence, more self-reliance, improved learning rate and a happier, more loving relationship with you.

Notes on the Lectures • In the rush of excitement following the release of *Dianetics: The Modern Science of Mental Health*,

L. Ron Hubbard was in demand all over the world as a speaker. This book is compiled from his fascinating lectures given right after the publication of *Dianetics: The Modern Science of Mental Health*. In them, he expands on the powerful principles of Dianetics and its application to groups.

Basic Scientology Books

Scientology: The Fundamentals of Thought • Improve life *and* make a better world with this easy-to-read book that lays out the fundamental truths about life and thought. No such knowledge has ever before existed, and no such results have ever before been attainable as those which can be reached by the use of this knowledge. Equipped with this book alone, one could perform seeming miracles in changing the states of health, ability and intelligence of people. This *is* how life works. This *is* how you change men, women and children for the better, and attain greater personal freedom.

A New Slant on Life • Have you ever asked yourself who am I? What am I? This book of articles by L. Ron Hubbard answers these all too common questions. This is knowledge one can use every day—for a new, more confident and happier slant on life!

The Problems of Work • Work plays a big part in the game of life. Do you really enjoy your work? Are you certain of your job security? Would you like the increased personal satisfaction of doing your work well? This is the book that shows exactly how to achieve these things and more. The game of life—and within it, the game of work—can be enjoyable and rewarding.

Scientology 0-8: The Book of Basics • What is life? Did you know an individual can create space, energy and time? Here are the basics of life itself, and the secrets of becoming cause over any area of your life. Discover how you can use the data in this book to achieve your goals.

Books on the Purification Program

Purification: An Illustrated Answer to Drugs • Do toxins and drugs hold down your ability to think clearly? What is the Purification Program and how does it work? How can harmful chemical substances be gotten out of the body? Our society is ridden by abuse of drugs, alcohol and medicine that reduce one's ability to think clearly. Find out what can be done in this introduction to the Purification Program.

All About Radiation • Can the effects of radiation exposure be avoided or reduced? What exactly would happen in the event of an atomic explosion? Get the answers to these and many other questions in this illuminating book. *All About Radiation* describes observations and discoveries concerning the physical and mental effects of radiation and the possibilities for handling them. Get the real facts on the subject of radiation and its effects.

Books on Past Lives

Have You Lived Before This Life? • This is the book that sparked a flood of interest in the ancient puzzle: Does man live only one life? The answer lay in mystery, buried until L. Ron Hubbard's researches unearthed the truth. Actual case histories of people recalling past lives in auditing tell the tale.

Mission Into Time • Here is a fascinating account of a unique research expedition into both space and time, locating physical evidence of past lives in an area rich with history—the Mediterranean.

Advanced Scientology Books

Scientology 8-8008 • Get the basic truths about your nature as a spiritual being and your relationship to the physical universe around you. Here, L. Ron Hubbard describes procedures designed to increase your abilities to heights previously only dreamed of.

Scientology 8-80 • What are the laws of life? We are all familiar with physical laws such as the law of gravity, but what laws govern life and thought? L. Ron Hubbard answers the riddles of life and its goals in the physical universe.

Scientology: A History of Man • A cold-blooded and factual account of the ancient background and history of the human race—revolutionary concepts guaranteed to intrigue you and challenge many basic assumptions about man's true power, potential and abilities.

The Phoenix Lectures • An in-depth look at the roots of Scientology religious philosophy and how it was developed is contained in this work. The influence of earlier great philosophies and religious leaders is covered in detail. This is followed by a complete discussion of the nature of existence and reality, and exactly how man interacts with his environment. An enlightening look at the infinite potentialities of man.

The Creation of Human Ability • Improve your life, and the lives of others, far beyond current expectations. Learn simple yet powerful techniques you can use to help somebody increase their ability and operate more successfully in life.

Handbook for Preclears • This personal workbook contains easily done exercises to help you improve your life and find greater happiness.

Advanced Procedure and Axioms • For the *first* time the basics of thought and the physical universe have been codified into a set of fundamental laws, signaling an entire new way to view and approach the subjects of man, the physical universe and even life itself.

Dictionaries

Basic Dictionary of Dianetics and Scientology • Compiled from the works of L. Ron Hubbard, this convenient dictionary contains the terms and expressions needed by anyone learning Dianetics and Scientology technology. And a *special bonus*—an easy-to-read Scientology Organizing Board chart that shows you who to contact for services and information at your nearest Scientology Organization.

Dianetics and Scientology Technical Dictionary • This dictionary is your indispensable guide to the words and ideas of Scientology and Dianetics technologies—technologies which can help you increase your know-how and effectiveness in life. Over three thousand words are defined—including a new understanding of vital words like *life, love* and *happiness* as well as Scientology terms.

Modern Management Technology Defined: Hubbard Dictionary of Administration and Management • Here's a real breakthrough in the subject of administration and management! Eighty-six hundred words are defined for greater understanding of any business situation. Clear, precise Scientology definitions describe many previously baffling phenomena and bring truth, sanity and understanding to the often murky field of business management.

Basic Executive Books

How to Live Though an Executive • What is the one factor in business and commerce which, if lacking, can keep a person overworked and worried, keep labor and management at each other's throats, and make an unsafe working atmosphere? L. Ron Hubbard reveals principles based on years of research into many different types of organizations.

Introduction to Scientology Ethics • Find out how to improve conditions in life and reach higher states of awareness and survival in one's job, family and life. Here's a practical book to be applied in all aspects of your life. *Introduction to Scientology Ethics* explains how to live a more honest and ethical life. Here is a practical system for helping you achieve your goals.

Graduate Executive Books

Organization Executive Course • The *Organization Executive Course* volumes contain workable organizational technology never before known to man. This is not just how a Scientology organization works; this is how the operation of *any* organization, *any* activity, can be improved. A person knowing the data in these volumes fully, and applying it, could completely reverse any downtrend in a company—or even a country!

Management Series Volume 1 • Never before has such a collection of state-of-the-art management technology been available for instant use. This large volume gives you the secrets of organizing anything to flow smoothly and efficiently with increased production and viability.

Management Series Volume 2 • Here is high-tech for any business executive or manager. In this 768-page volume you get down to the basics of finance, personnel, marketing and public relations. Get powerful data to strategically plan and coordinate so you can accomplish any objective. Learn how to be a powerful, effective executive and stay one.

Reference Materials

Background and Ceremonies of the Church of Scientology • Discover the beautiful and inspiring ceremonies of the Church of Scientology, and its fascinating religious and historical background. This book contains the illuminating Creed of the Church,

church services, sermons and ceremonies, many as originally given in person by L. Ron Hubbard, Founder of Scientology.

What is Scientology? • Scientology applied religious philosophy has attracted great interest and attention since its beginning. What is Scientology philosophy? What can it accomplish—and why are so many people from all walks of life proclaiming its effectiveness? Find the answers to these questions and many others in *What is Scientology?*

Books to Help You Counsel Others

Introductory and Demonstration Processes and Assists • How can you help someone increase his enthusiasm for living? How can you improve someone's self-confidence on the job? Here are basic Scientology processes you can use to help others deal with life and living.

Volunteer Minister's Handbook • This is a big, practical how-to-do-it book to give a person the basic knowledge on how to help self and others through the rough spots in life. It consists of twenty-one sections—each one covering important situations in life, such as drug and alcohol problems, study difficulties, broken marriages, accidents and illnesses, a failing business, difficult children, and much more. This is the basic tool with which to help someone out of troubles, and bring about a happier life.

The Classic Cassettes Series

There are nearly three thousand recorded lectures by L. Ron Hubbard on the subjects of Dianetics and Scientology. What follows is a sampling of these lectures, each known and loved the world over. All of the Classic Cassettes are presented in Clearsound state-of-the-art sound-recording technology, notable for its clarity and brilliance of reproduction.

The Dianetics Lecture Series • These four lectures were given by Ron in the months following the publication of *Dianetics: The Modern Science of Mental Health* in 1950. He lectured about Dianetics technology and how to use it in life, how to handle preclears and what a Dianetics auditor is responsible for.

The Story of Dianetics and Scientology • In this lecture, L. Ron Hubbard shares with you his earliest insights into human nature and gives a compelling and often humorous account of his experiences. Spend an unforgettable time with Ron as he talks about the start of Dianetics and Scientology!

The Road to Truth • The road to truth has eluded man since the beginning of time. In this classic lecture, L. Ron Hubbard explains what this road actually is and why it is the only road one MUST travel all the way once begun. This lecture reveals the only road to higher levels of living.

Scientology and Effective Knowledge • Voyage to new horizons of awareness! *Scientology and Effective Knowledge* by L. Ron Hubbard can help you understand more about yourself and others. A fascinating tale of the beginnings of Dianetics and Scientology.

My Philosophy • Three dramatic essays written by Ron— "My Philosophy," "The Aims of Scientology" and "A Description of Scientology"—come alive for you in this cassette. These powerful writings, beautifully read and set to new and inspiring music, tell you what Scientology is, what it does and what its aims are.

More advanced books and lectures are available. Contact your nearest organization or write directly to the publisher for a full catalog.

Learn how to USE Dianetics technology at a hands-on *Dianetics Seminar*

We were all born with a mental computer far more sophisticated than the most advanced computers in the world today. However, we are not trained in how to USE this incredible computer to solve our problems and worries and unblock our full natural capacity.

Now in just one weekend (or five evenings), you can get practical hands-on experience in handling this amazing computer and using Dianetics technology to better your life. The *Hubbard Dianetics Seminar* is designed to give you an introduction to Dianetics principles and techniques, on an easy, enjoyable gradient.

People who have done the *Hubbard Dianetics Seminar* have reported:

- Return of enthusiasm for life
- Increased self-confidence
- The ability to instantly help someone else

  —*and much more!*

Don't put up with the stresses, worries and upsets in life any longer. Start on the road to a happier life with the *Hubbard Dianetics Seminar*.

Start today!

Contact the Public Registrar at your nearest Hubbard Dianetics Foundation.

(A complete list of Hubbard Dianetics Foundations is provided at the back of this book.)

Begin a better life with Dianetics Extension Courses

Dianetics books by L. Ron Hubbard provide the knowledge needed to understand and use the world's most incredible computer—your own mind. Now learn to *use* that knowledge to gain greater happiness and self-confidence in life. Enroll on a Dianetics Extension Course.

Each extension course package includes a lesson booklet with easy-to-understand instructions and all the lessons you will need to complete it. Each course can be done in the comfort of your own home or right in your local Hubbard Dianetics Foundation. Your Extension Course Supervisor will review each lesson as you complete it (or mail it in if you do the course at home) and get the results right back to you. When you complete the course you get a beautiful certificate, suitable for framing.

The Dynamics of Life
Extension Course

Based on L. Ron Hubbard's concise introduction to the subject of Dianetics. This course takes you through L. Ron Hubbard's first book on the subject and helps to teach you the basics of the mind and how it *really* works. Order your copy today!

Self Analysis
Extension Course

How good can you get? How much can you improve your life? The *Self Analysis Extension Course* takes you through the book *Self Analysis* and helps you get a full understanding and ability to apply the materials in it. *Self Analysis* is a complete do-it-yourself manual for personal improvement, and this home study course will get you the maximum benefits from the exercises contained in this book. Order your copy today!

The Dianetics Extension Course

Based on the book *Dianetics: The Modern Science of Mental Health,* this course takes you step-by-step through the book, helping you to understand each part as you go along. The lessons pinpoint key data in the book. You'll learn about Clear, the reactive mind, the analytical mind and the complete technology of Dianetics. Order your copy today!

Dianetics: The Evolution of a Science Extension Course

Based on L. Ron Hubbard's introduction to Dianetics, this course will help you gain a basic understanding of the principles and techniques of Dianetics. You'll also get a better understanding of how L. Ron Hubbard discovered the principles of Dianetics, and how he developed the techniques that are used today around the world to create happier, more successful lives. Order your copy today!

Enroll on a Dianetics Extension Course Today!

For information and enrollment and prices for these Extension Courses and the books they accompany, contact the Public Registrar at your nearest Hubbard Dianetics Foundation. (A complete list of Hubbard Dianetics Foundations is provided at the back of this book.)

Get Your Free Catalog of Knowledge on How to Improve Life

L. Ron Hubbard's books and tapes increase your ability to understand yourself and others. His works give you the practical know-how you need to improve your life and the lives of your family and friends.

Many more materials by L. Ron Hubbard are available than have been covered in the pages of this book. A free catalog of these materials is available on request.

Write for your free catalog today!

Bridge Publications, Inc.
4751 Fountain Avenue
Los Angeles, California 90029

New Era Publications International, ApS
Store Kongensgade 55
1264 Copenhagen K, Denmark

For more information about Dianetics or to order books and cassettes

---

Call: **1-800-367-8788**
in the U.S. and Canada

Is there such a thing as a hotline that doesn't believe in giving advice? What about a hotline for able individuals to help them solve their *own* problems?

"If we take a man and keep giving him advice," L. Ron Hubbard has said, "we don't necessarily wind up with a resolution of his problems. But if, on the other hand, we put him in a position where he had higher intelligence, where his reaction time was better, where he could confront life better, where he could identify the factors in his life more easily, then he's in a position where he can solve his own problems."

Call the unique new hotline and referral service with operators trained in Dianetics technology. Callers find someone they can trust to talk to about a problem, and they are referred to their nearest Hubbard Dianetics Foundation for more information if they are interested.

You can also order books and cassettes by L. Ron Hubbard by calling this number.

Call this toll-free number
7 days a week
from 9 A.M. to 11 P.M. Pacific Standard Time.

"I am always happy to hear from my readers."

L. Ron Hubbard

These were the words of L. Ron Hubbard, who was always very interested in hearing from his friends, readers and followers. He made a point of staying in communication with everyone he came in contact with over his fifty-year career as a professional writer, and he had thousands of fans and friends that he corresponded with all over the world.

The publishers of L. Ron Hubbard's literary works wish to continue this tradition and would welcome letters and comments from you, his readers, both old and new.

Any message addressed to the Author's Affairs Director at Bridge Publications will be given prompt and full attention.

Bridge Publications, Inc.
4751 Fountain Avenue
Los Angeles, California 90029
U.S.A.

Address List

UNITED STATES OF AMERICA

Albuquerque
Hubbard Dianetics Foundation
1210 San Pedro NE
Albuquerque, New Mexico 87110

Ann Arbor
Hubbard Dianetics Foundation
301 North Ingalls Street
Ann Arbor, Michigan 48104

Austin
Hubbard Dianetics Foundation
2200 Guadalupe
Austin, Texas 78705

Boston
Hubbard Dianetics Foundation
448 Beacon Street
Boston, Massachusetts 02115

Buffalo
Hubbard Dianetics Foundation
47 West Huron Street
Buffalo, New York 14202

Chicago
Hubbard Dianetics Foundation
3009 North Lincoln Avenue
Chicago, Illinois 60657

Cincinnati
Hubbard Dianetics Foundation
215 West 4th Street, 5th Floor
Cincinnati, Ohio 45202

Clearwater
Hubbard Dianetics Foundation
210 South Fort Harrison Avenue
Clearwater, Florida 33516

Columbus
Hubbard Dianetics Foundation
167 East State Street
Columbus, Ohio 43215

Dallas
Hubbard Dianetics Foundation
Celebrity Centre Dallas
8501 Manderville Lane
Dallas, Texas 75231

Denver
Hubbard Dianetics Foundation
375 South Navajo Street
Denver, Colorado 80223

Detroit
Hubbard Dianetics Foundation
321 Williams Street
Royal Oak, Michigan 48067

Honolulu
Hubbard Dianetics Foundation
1100 Alakea Street #301
Honolulu, Hawaii 96813

Kansas City
Hubbard Dianetics Foundation
3742 Broadway, Suite 203
Kansas City, Missouri 64111

Las Vegas
Hubbard Dianetics Foundation
846 East Sahara Avenue
Las Vegas, Nevada 89104

Hubbard Dianetics Foundation
Celebrity Centre Las Vegas
1100 South 10th Street
Las Vegas, Nevada 89104

Long Island
Hubbard Dianetics Foundation
330 Fulton Avenue
Hempstead, New York 11550

Los Angeles
Hubbard Dianetics Foundation
4810 Sunset Boulevard
Los Angeles, California 90027

Hubbard Dianetics Foundation
1306 North Berendo Street
Los Angeles, California 90027

Hubbard Dianetics Foundation
1413 North Berendo Street
Los Angeles, California 90027

Hubbard Dianetics Foundation
Celebrity Centre International
5930 Franklin Avenue
Hollywood, California 90028

Miami
Hubbard Dianetics Foundation
120 Giralda Avenue
Coral Gables, Florida 33134

Minneapolis
Hubbard Dianetics Foundation
3019 Minnehaha Avenue
Minneapolis, Minnesota 55406

New Haven
Hubbard Dianetics Foundation
909 Whalley Avenue
New Haven, Connecticut 06515

New York City
Hubbard Dianetics Foundation
227 West 46th Street
New York City, New York 10036

Hubbard Dianetics Foundation
Celebrity Centre New York
65 East 82nd Street
New York City, New York 10028

Orange County
Hubbard Dianetics Foundation
1451 Irvine Boulevard
Tustin, California 92680

Orlando
Hubbard Dianetics Foundation
710-A East Colonial Drive
Orlando, Florida 32803

Pasadena
Hubbard Dianetics Foundation
263 East Colorado Boulevard
Pasadena, California 91101

Philadelphia
Hubbard Dianetics Foundation
1315 Race Street
Philadelphia, Pennsylvania 19107

Phoenix
Hubbard Dianetics Foundation
4450 North Central Avenue, Suite 102
Phoenix, Arizona 85012

Portland
Hubbard Dianetics Foundation
1536 South East 11th Avenue
Portland, Oregon 97214

Hubbard Dianetics Foundation
Celebrity Centre Portland
709 South West Salmon Street
Portland, Oregon 97205

Sacramento
Hubbard Dianetics Foundation
825 15th Street
Sacramento, California 95814

San Diego
Hubbard Dianetics Foundation
2409 Fourth Avenue
San Diego, California 92101

San Fernando Valley
Hubbard Dianetics Foundation
10335 Magnolia Boulevard
North Hollywood, California 91601

San Francisco
Hubbard Dianetics Foundation
91 McAllister Street
San Francisco, California 94102

San Jose
Hubbard Dianetics Foundation
3604 Stevens Creek Boulevard
San Jose, California 95117

Santa Barbara
Hubbard Dianetics Foundation
524 State Street
Santa Barbara, California 93101

Seattle
Hubbard Dianetics Foundation
2004 Westlake Avenue
Seattle, Washington 98121

St. Louis
Hubbard Dianetics Foundation
9510 Page Boulevard
St. Louis, Missouri 63132

Tampa
Hubbard Dianetics Foundation
4809 North Armenia Avenue, Suite 215
Tampa, Florida 33603

Washington, D.C.
Hubbard Dianetics Foundation
2125 "S" Street N.W.
Washington, D.C. 20008

CANADA

Edmonton
Hubbard Dianetics Foundation
10349 82nd Avenue
Edmonton, Alberta
Canada T6E 1Z9

Kitchener
Hubbard Dianetics Foundation
8 Water Street North
Kitchener, Ontario
Canada N2H 5A5

Montreal
Centre de Dianétique Hubbard
4489 Papineau Street
Montréal, Québec
Canada H2H 1T7

Ottawa
Hubbard Dianetics Foundation
150 Rideau Street, 2nd Floor
Ottawa, Ontario
Canada K1N 5X6

Québec
Centre de Dianétique Hubbard
226 St-Joseph est
Québec, Québec
Canada G1K 3A9

Toronto
Hubbard Dianetics Foundation
700 Yonge Street
Toronto, Ontario
Canada M4Y 2A7

Vancouver
Hubbard Dianetics Foundation
405 West Hastings Street
Vancouver, British Columbia
Canada V6B 1L5

Winnipeg
Hubbard Dianetics Foundation
Suite 125—388 Donald Street
Winnipeg, Manitoba
Canada R3B 2J4

UNITED KINGDOM

Birmingham
Hubbard Dianetics Foundation
80 Hurst Street
Birmingham
England B5 4TD

Brighton
Hubbard Dianetics Foundation
Dukes Arcade, Top Floor
Dukes Street
Brighton, Sussex
England

East Grinstead
Hubbard Dianetics Foundation
Saint Hill Manor
East Grinstead, West Sussex
England RH19 4JY

Edinburgh
Hubbard Dianetics Foundation
20 Southbridge
Edinburgh, Scotland EH1 1LL

London
Hubbard Dianetics Foundation
68 Tottenham Court Road
London, W1P 0BB England

Manchester
Hubbard Dianetics Foundation
258 Deansgate
Manchester, England M3 4BG

Plymouth
Hubbard Dianetics Foundation
41 Ebrington Street
Plymouth, Devon
England PL4 9AA

Sunderland
Hubbard Dianetics Foundation
51 Fawcett Street
Sunderland, Tyne and Wear
England SR1 1RS

AUSTRIA

Vienna
Hubbard Dianetics Foundation
Mariahilfer Strasse 88A/II/2
A-1070 Vienna, Austria

BELGIUM

Brussels
Hubbard Dianetics Foundation
45A, rue de l'Ecuyer
1000 Bruxelles, Belgium

DENMARK

Aarhus
Hubbard Dianetics Foundation
Guldsmedegade 17, 2
8000 Aarhus C., Denmark

Copenhagen
Hubbard Dianetics Foundation
Store Kongensgade 55
1264 Copenhagen K, Denmark

Hubbard Dianetics Foundation
Vesterbrogade 25
1620 Copenhagen V, Denmark

Hubbard Dianetics Foundation
Jernbanegade 6
1608 Copenhagen V, Denmark

FRANCE

Angers
Centre de Dianétique Hubbard
10–12, rue Max Richard
49000 Angers, France

Clermont-Ferrand
Centre de Dianétique Hubbard
2 Pte rue Giscard de la Tour Fondue
63000 Clermont-Ferrand, France

Lyon
Centre de Dianétique Hubbard
3, place des Capucins
69001 Lyon, France

Paris
Centre de Dianétique Hubbard
65, rue de Dunkerque
75009 Paris, France

Hubbard Dianetics Foundation
Celebrity Centre Paris
69, rue Legendre
75017 Paris, France

St. Etienne
Centre de Dianétique Hubbard
24 rue Marengo
42000 St. Etienne, France

GERMANY

Berlin
Hubbard Dianetics Foundation
Sponholzstrasse 51/52
1000 Berlin 41, Germany

Düsseldorf
Hubbard Dianetics Foundation
Friedrichstrasse 28
4000 Düsseldorf
West Germany

Frankfurt
Hubbard Dianetics Foundation
Darmstatter Landstrasse 119-125
6000 Frankfurt/Main
West Germany

Hamburg
Hubbard Dianetics Foundation
Steindamm 63
2000 Hamburg 1
West Germany

Hubbard Dianetics Foundation
Celebrity Centre Hamburg
Mönckebergstrasse 5
2000 Hamburg 1
West Germany

Munich
Hubbard Dianetics Foundation
Beichstrasse 12
D-8000 München 40
West Germany

GREECE

Athens
Hubbard Dianetics Foundation
Ippokratous 175B
114 72 Athens, Greece

ISRAEL

Tel Aviv
Hubbard Dianetics Foundation
7 Salomon Street
Tel Aviv 66023, Israel

ITALY

Brescia
Hubbard Dianetics Foundation
Dei Tre Laghi
Via Fratelli Bronzetti N. 20
25125 Brescia, Italy

Milano
Hubbard Dianetics Foundation
Via Abetone, 10
20137 Milano, Italy

Monza
Hubbard Dianetics Foundation
Via Cavour, 5
20052 Monza, Italy

Novara
Hubbard Dianetics Foundation
Corso Cavallotti No. 7
28100 Novara, Italy

Nuoro
Hubbard Dianetics Foundation
Corso Garibaldi, 108
08100 Nuoro, Italy

Padua
Hubbard Dianetics Foundation
Via Mameli, 1/5
35131 Padova, Italy

Pordenone
Hubbard Dianetics Foundation
Via Montereale, 10/C
33170 Pordenone, Italy

Rome
Hubbard Dianetics Foundation
Via di San Vito, 11
00185 Roma, Italy

Turin
Hubbard Dianetics Foundation
Via Guarini, 4
10121 Torino, Italy

Verona
Hubbard Dianetics Foundation
Vicolo Chiodo No. 4/A
37121 Verona, Italy

NETHERLANDS

Amsterdam
Hubbard Dianetics Foundation
Nieuwe Zijds Voorburgwal 271
1012 RL Amsterdam, Netherlands

NORWAY

Oslo
Hubbard Dianetics Foundation
Storgata 9
0155 Oslo 1, Norway

PORTUGAL

Lisbon
Instituto de Dianética
Rua Actor Taborda 39–4°
1000 Lisboa, Portugal

SPAIN

Barcelona
Dianética
Calle Pau Claris 85, Principal 1ª
08010 Barcelona, Spain

Madrid
Asociación Civil de Dianética
Montera 20, Piso 1° dcha
28013 Madrid, Spain

SWEDEN

Göteborg
Hubbard Dianetics Foundation
Norra Hamngatan 4
S-411 14 Göteborg, Sweden

Malmö
Hubbard Dianetics Foundation
Stortorget 27
S-211 34 Malmö, Sweden

Stockholm
Hubbard Dianetics Foundation
Kammakargatan 46
S-111 60 Stockholm, Sweden

SWITZERLAND

Basel
Hubbard Dianetics Foundation
Herrengrabenweg 56
4054 Basel, Switzerland

Bern
Hubbard Dianetics Foundation
Effingerstrasse 25
P.O. Box 2188
CH-3008 Bern, Switzerland

Geneva
Hubbard Dianetics Foundation
4, rue du Léman
1201 Genève, Switzerland

Lausanne
Hubbard Dianetics Foundation
10, rue de la Madeleine
1003 Lausanne, Switzerland

Zürich
Hubbard Dianetics Foundation
Badenerstrasse 294
CH-8004 Zürich, Switzerland

AUSTRALIA

Adelaide
Hubbard Dianetics Foundation
24 Waymouth Street
Adelaide, South Australia 5000
Australia

Brisbane
Hubbard Dianetics Foundation
2nd Floor, 106 Edward Street
Brisbane, Queensland 4000
Australia

Canberra
Hubbard Dianetics Foundation
Suite 16, 1st Floor
108 Bunda Street
Civic, Canberra
A.C.T. 2601, Australia

Melbourne
Hubbard Dianetics Foundation
44 Russell Street
Melbourne, Victoria 3000
Australia

Perth
Hubbard Dianetics Foundation
39-41 King Street
Perth, Western Australia 6000
Australia

Sydney
Hubbard Dianetics Foundation
201 Castlereagh Street
Sydney, New South Wales 2000
Australia

Hubbard Dianetics Foundation
19-37 Greek Street
Glebe, New South Wales 2037
Australia

JAPAN

Tokyo
Hubbard Dianetics Foundation
101 Toyomi Nishi Gotanda Heights
2-13-5 Nishi Gotanda
Shinagawa-Ku
Tokyo, Japan 141

NEW ZEALAND

Auckland
Hubbard Dianetics Foundation
2nd Floor, 44 Queen Street
Auckland 1, New Zealand

AFRICA

Bulawayo
Hubbard Dianetics Foundation
74 Abercorn Street
Bulawayo, Zimbabwe

Cape Town
Hubbard Dianetics Foundation
5 Beckham Street
Gardens
Cape Town 8001, South Africa

Durban
Hubbard Dianetics Foundation
57 College Lane
Durban 4001, South Africa

Harare
Hubbard Dianetics Foundation
First Floor, State Lottery Building
Corner Julius Nyerere Way/Speke
  Avenue
P.O. Box 3524
Harare, Zimbabwe

Johannesburg
Hubbard Dianetics Foundation
Security Building, 1st Floor
95 Commissioner Street
Johannesburg 2001, South Africa

Hubbard Dianetics Foundation
101 Huntford Building
40 Hunter Street
Cnr. Hunter & Fortesque Roads
Yeoville 2198
Johannesburg, South Africa

Port Elizabeth
Hubbard Dianetics Foundation
2 St. Christopher
27 Westbourne Road
Port Elizabeth 6001, South Africa

Pretoria
Hubbard Dianetics Foundation
"Die Meent Arcade,"
  2nd Level, Shop 43b
266 Pretorius Street
Pretoria 0002, South Africa

COLOMBIA

Bogotá
Centro Cultural de Dianética
Carrera 19 No. 39–55
Apartado Aereo 92419
Bogotá, D.E. Colombia

MEXICO

Estado de México
Instituto Tecnologico de Dianética,
  A.C.
Reforma 530, Lomas
México D.F., C.P. 11000

Guadalajara
Organización Cultural Dianética de
  Guadalajara, A.C.
Av. Lopez Mateos Nte.
329 Sector Hidalgo
Guadalajara, Jalisco, México

Mexico City
Asociación Cultural Dianética, A.C.
Hermes No. 46
Colonia Crédito Constructor
03940 México 19, D.F.

Instituto de Filosofia Aplicada, A.C.
Durango 105
Colonia Roma
06700 México D.F.

Instituto de Filosofia Aplicada, A.C.
Plaza Rio de Janeiro No. 52
Colonia Roma
06700 México D.F.

Organización, Desarrollo y Dianética,
  A.C.
Providencia 1000
Colonia Del Valle
C.P. 03100 México D.F.

Centro de Dianética Polanco
Insurgentes Sur 536 1er piso Esq.
Nogales
Colonia Roma Sur C.P.
06700 México D.F.

VENEZUELA

Valencia
Asociación Cultural Dianética de
  Venezuela, A.C.
Ave. 101 No. 150–23
Urbanizacion La Alegria
Apartado Postal 833
Valencia, Venezuela

To obtain any books or cassettes by L. Ron Hubbard which are not available at your local organization, contact any of the following publishers:

UNITED STATES OF AMERICA
Bridge Publications, Inc.
4751 Fountain Avenue
Los Angeles, California 90029

CANADA
Continental Publications Liaison Office
696 Yonge Street
Toronto, Ontario M4Y 2A7

DENMARK
NEW ERA Publications
   International ApS
Store Kongensgade 55
1264 Copenhagen K

MEXICO
Era Dinámica Editores, S.A. de C.V.
Alabama 105
Colonia Nápoles
C.P. 03810 México, D.F.

UNITED KINGDOM
NEW ERA Publications, Ltd.
78 Holmethorpe Avenue
Redhill, Surrey RH1 2NL

AUSTRALIA
N.E. Publications Australia Pty. Ltd.
2 Verona Street
Paddington, New South Wales 2021

AFRICA
Continental Publications Pty. Ltd.
P.O. Box 27080
Benrose 2011
South Africa

ITALY
NEW ERA Publications Italia Srl
Via L. G. Columella, 12
20128 Milano

GERMANY
NEW ERA Publications GmbH
Otto—Hahn—Strasse 25
6072 Dreieich 1

FRANCE
NEW ERA Publications France
111, Boulevard de Magenta
75010 Paris

SPAIN
New Era Publications España, S.A.
C/De la Paz, 4/1° dcha
28012 Madrid

JAPAN
NEW ERA—Japan
5-4-5-803 Nishigotanda
Shinagawa—Ku
Tokyo, Japan 141